JAMESTOWN PUBLISHERS

THE WILD SIDE

Extreme Sports

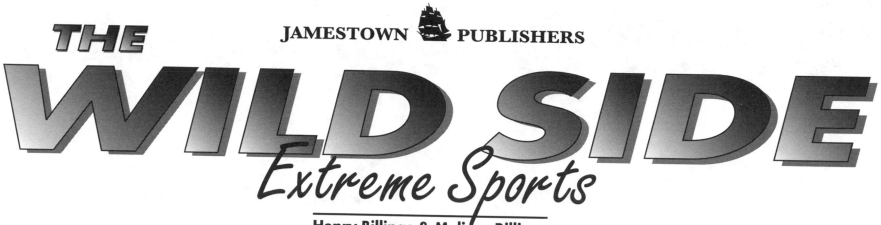

JAMESTOWN PUBLISHERS

THE WILD SIDE
Extreme Sports

Henry Billings & Melissa Billings

JAMESTOWN PUBLISHERS

a division of NTC/CONTEMPORARY PUBLISHING COMPANY
Lincolnwood, Illinois USA

Photo Credits
Adventure Photo & Film: 1,4/Renee Vernon, 48/Didier Giviois,
48/Gary Sanders Brettnacher, 92/Tom; UPI/Corbis-Bettman: 41, 44,
60, 73, 76; Libero Di Zinno Photographs: 98/Tony Di Zinno;
Image Bank: 66, 86

ISBN: 0-89061-800 3

Published by Jamestown Publishers,
a division of NTC/Contemporary Publishing Company,
4255 West Touhy Avenue,
Lincolnwood (Chicago), Illinois 60646-1975 U.S.A.

Executive Editor	*Production Artist*
Marilyn Cunningham	Thomas D. Scharf
Design and Production Manager	*Electronic Composition*
Norma Underwood	Victoria A. Randall
Cover Design	*Cover Illustration*
Michael Kelly	Tim Jessell

Contents

To the Teacher   **vii**

    Introduction

    How to Use This Book

    Related Texts

Sample Unit: Street Luge: Fast, Fun, . . . Dangerous!   **2**

To the Student   **8**

GROUP ONE

Unit 1   The Human Fly   **10**

Unit 2   Bungee Jumping: A Leap of Faith   **16**

Unit 3   White Water Thrills   **22**

Unit 4   Hang Gliding: Riding the Wind   **28**

Unit 5   Climbing the World's Highest Mountains   **34**

GROUP TWO

Unit 6   The World's Wildest Horse Race   **42**

Unit 7   Skiing the Impossible   **48**

Unit 8   Running with the Bulls   **54**

Unit 9   Stunt Flying   **60**

Unit 10   The Last Great Race on Earth   **66**

GROUP THREE

Unit 11   Conquering Niagara Falls   **74**

Unit 12   Evel Knievel: Motorcycle Maniac   **80**

Unit 13   Buzkashi: War on Horseback   **86**

Unit 14   BASE Jumping: The Outer Edge of Danger   **92**

Unit 15   Raid Gauloises: Ten Days of Hell   **98**

Answer Key   **106**

Words-per-Minute Tables   **110**

Progress Graphs

    Reading Speed   **113**

    Critical Reading Scores   **114**

To the Teacher

INTRODUCTION

Sports are important to us in many ways. Participation in sports, whether individual or team activities, contributes to good health. Cooperative skills learned in team sports are applicable throughout life. Even as observers, we feel pride in those who represent us in competitions. Extreme sports, however, are a different matter. An extreme sportsperson is less interested in improving his or her body than in challenging it, pushing it to its limits. He or she is less interested in winning or losing than in overcoming fear and doing what others said couldn't be done. The pride that an extreme athlete feels is often beyond the understanding of the general public, which may see little point to the risks that extreme sports present. In *Extreme Sports*, you and your students will discover a world of excitement and challenge that will impress and startle you.

Extreme Sports provides subject matter for thoughtful interpretation and discussion, while challenging your students in four critical reading categories: main idea, important details, inferences, and vocabulary in context. *Extreme Sports* can also help your students improve their reading rates. Timed reading of the selections is optional, but many teachers find this an effective motivating device.

Extreme Sports consists of fifteen units divided into three groups of five units each. All the stories in a group are on the same reading level. Group One is at the fourth-grade reading level, Group Two at the fifth, and Group Three at the sixth, as assessed by the Fry Formula for Estimating Readability.

HOW TO USE THIS BOOK

Introducing the Book. This text, used creatively, can be an effective tool for teaching certain critical reading skills. We suggest that you begin by introducing the students to the contents and format of the book. Discuss the title. What makes some sports "extreme"? Encourage students to think of dangerous sports and stunts they have heard of or read about. What drives people to pursue such activities, even if it means risking their lives? Ask your students to recall extreme sports, athletes, and feats that have become topics of conversation across the country and around the world. Then read through the table of contents as a class to gain an overview of the topics that will be encountered in *Extreme Sports*.

The Sample Unit. Turn to the Sample Unit on pages 2–7. After you have examined these pages yourself, work through the Sample Unit with your students, so that they have a clear understanding of the purpose of the book and of how they are to use it.

The Sample Unit is set up exactly as the fifteen regular units are. The introductory page includes a photograph or illustration accompanied by a brief introduction to the story. The next two pages contain the story and are followed by four types of comprehension exercises: Finding the Main Idea, Recalling Facts, Making Inferences, and Using Words Precisely.

Begin by having someone in the class read aloud the introduction. Then give the students a few moments to study the picture. Ask them to predict what the story will be about. Continue the discussion for a minute or so. Then have the students read the story. (You may wish to time the students' reading in order to help them increase their reading speed and improve their comprehension. Students can use the Words-per-Minute tables located on pages 110–112 to help them figure their reading speed.)

Work through the sample exercises with the class. At the beginning of each exercise are an explanation of the comprehension skill and directions for answering the questions. Make sure all the students understand how to complete the four different types of exercises and how to determine their scores. The correct answers for the exercises and sample scores are printed in lighter type. Also, explanations of the correct answers are given for the sample Finding the Main Idea and Making Inferences exercises to help the students understand how to think through these question types.

As the students work through the Sample Unit, have them turn to the Words-per-Minute table on page 110 (if you have timed their reading) and the Reading Speed and Critical Reading Scores graphs on pages 113 and 114 at the appropriate points. Explain the purpose of each feature and read the directions with the students. Be sure they understand how to use the tables and graphs. You may need to help them find and mark their scores for the first several units.

Timing the Story. If you choose to time your students' reading, explain your reason for doing so: to help them track and increase their reading speed.

One way to time the reading is to have all the students in the class begin reading the story at the same time. After one minute has passed, write on the chalkboard the time that has elapsed. Update the time at ten-second intervals (1:00, 1:10, 1:20, etc.). Tell the students to copy down the last time shown on the chalkboard when they finish reading. They should then record this reading time in the space designated after the story.

Have the students use the Words-per-Minute tables to check their reading rates. They should then enter their reading speed on the Reading Speed graph on page 113. Graphing their reading times allows the students to keep track of increases in their reading speed.

Working Through Each Unit. When the students have carefully completed all parts of the Sample Unit, they should be ready to tackle the regular units. Begin each unit by having someone in the class read aloud the introduction to the story, just as you did in the Sample Unit. Discuss the topic of the story and allow the students time to study the illustration.

Then have the students read the story. If you are timing the reading, have the students enter their reading time, find their reading speed, and record their speed on the Reading Speed graph after they have finished reading the story.

Next, direct the students to complete the four comprehension exercises without looking back at the story. When they have finished, go over the questions and answers with them. Have the students grade their own answers and make the necessary corrections. Then have them enter their Critical Reading Scores on the graph on page 114.

The Graphs. Students enjoy graphing their work. Graphs show, in a concrete and easily understandable way, how a student is progressing. Seeing a line of progressively rising scores gives students the incentive to continue striving for improvement.

Check the graphs regularly. This will allow you to establish a routine for reviewing each student's progress. Discuss with each student what the graphs show and what kind of progress you expect. Establish guidelines and warning signals so that students will know when to approach you for counseling and advice.

RELATED TEXTS

If you find that your students enjoy and benefit from the stories and skills exercises in *Extreme Sports*, you may be interested in *Weird Science*, *Crime and Punishment*, *Angry Animals*, *Bizarre Endings*, and *Total Panic*—five related Jamestown texts. All feature high-interest stories and work in four critical reading comprehension skills. As in *Extreme Sports*, the units in those books are divided into three groups, at reading levels four, five, and six.

Most skateboards are about the size of a person's foot, but some have grown. These young athletes share a ride on a board about four feet long. This long board looks somewhat like the sled used in a winter sport called luge. In winter luge, riders lie flat on their backs on the sled and speed feetfirst down an ice-covered hill. In street luge, riders lie on their backs on an extra-long skateboard, like this one, and speed feetfirst down city streets. Broken bones and scraped skin are an unavoidable part of this sport.

STREET LUGE: FAST, FUN, . . . DANGEROUS!

Going really fast is easy. Any top street luge racer can hit sixty miles per hour or more. The tricky part is slowing down. If you do it well, you can smile and race again. If not, that cracking sound you hear will be your bones!

Street luge racing is becoming more and more popular in the United States. It's a great test of speed and skill. But it's also very dangerous. The idea is to race down a hill while lying on a skateboard. The skateboard is extralong, but it has no padding. And believe it or not, it has no brakes.

To race, street lugers lie down on the skateboards. They lie on their backs with their feet in front. That puts them just a few inches off the road. They steer by leaning to the left or the right. They have to know exactly how to position their bodies when heading into a curve. Turning too much or too little will send a skateboard flying off the course. It's no wonder street lugers are sometimes called pilots!

Street luge is not done on a special track. Instead, racers use regular streets. Although they wait until these streets have been closed to traffic, many hazards remain. Sidewalks, street signs, and telephone poles all pose threats to the racers. And that's not all. Some race courses have ninety-degree turns in the middle. Any racer who fails to make the turn is bound to crash into something hard.

Stopping without brakes can be a real challenge. Racers must use their feet as brakes. They drag them hard on the asphalt. Often they dig in with such force that they leave skid marks. They send smoke and the smell of burning rubber into the air.

Racers need some kind of protection for their bodies. They wear helmets, elbow pads, and leather clothing. Still, sooner or later anyone who races will get hurt. Bob Pereyra is a top street luger. He broke both ankles in one crash. In another accident, he broke three ribs. And in a bad practice run in 1995, he fractured his heel in three places. Roger Hickey is also a top racer. Over his career, he has broken more than fifty bones. He says he has also left enough skin on the road "to make a mannequin."

If the pros get this banged up, what happens to rookies? Darren Lott, author of *Street Luge Survival Guide*, writes about one young daredevil named Zac Bernstein. At the age of twenty-one, Zac knew no fear. He took to street luge quickly. He wanted to go faster and faster on every run. On one steep hill, he took a turn a bit wide. He went bouncing into a field and hit a storm drain. He smashed right into the concrete wall on the far side of the drain.

Without his helmet, Zac would have died. Even with it, he broke lots of bones and slit open his throat. Zac spent weeks in the hospital recovering. But just one month after the accident, he was back racing again. He had pins in his hip and leg and walked with a cane. But he was not ready to give up the sport he loved.

Street luge has been around for years. No one person "invented" it. Instead, the sport caught on in several places more or less at the same time. Darren Lott writes, "In the 1970s we were constantly running into little groups that thought they were the only ones in the world doing it." That has changed. Today street luge is getting lots of attention. It has even

shown up on TV sports shows. Still, as long as there are people like Zac Bernstein around, street luge will remain a truly extreme sport.

If you have been timed while reading this selection, enter your reading time on the right. Then turn to the Words-per-Minute table on page 110 and look up your reading speed (words per minute). When you are working through the regular units, you will then enter your reading speed on the graph on page 113.

READING TIME: Sample Unit
_____ : _____
Minutes   *Seconds*

This street luger is in position and ready to race. A helmet is a must in this dangerous sport.

How Well Did You Read?

• *The four types of exercises that follow appear in each unit of this book. The directions for each type of exercise tell you how to mark your answers. In this Sample Unit, the answers are marked for you. Also, for the Finding the Main Idea and Making Inferences exercises, explanations of the answers are given to help you understand how to think through these question types. Read through these exercises carefully.*

• *When you have finished all four exercises in a unit, use the answer key that starts on page 106 to check your work. For each right answer, put a check mark (✓) on the line beside the box. For each wrong answer, write the correct answer on the line.*

• *Find your scores by following the directions after each exercise. In this unit, sample scores are entered as examples.*

A FINDING THE MAIN IDEA

A good main idea statement answers two questions: it tells *who* or *what* is the subject of the story, and it answers the understood question *does what?* or *is what?* Look at the three statements below. One expresses the main idea of the story you just read. Another statement is *too broad*; it is vague and doesn't tell much about the topic of the story. The third statement is *too narrow*; it tells about only one part of the story.

Match the statements with the three answer choices below by writing the letter of each answer in the box in front of the statement it goes with.

M—Main Idea   **B—Too Broad**   **N—Too Narrow**

✓ [B] 1. Street luge often results in injury to the athletes who take part in it.
[This statement is *too broad*. It doesn't give a clear idea of the sport that the story is about.]

✓ [M] 2. Street luge racers, who speed down streets lying on long skateboards without brakes, love the sport despite frequent injuries.
[This statement is the *main idea*. It describes what happens in street luge and how lugers feel about the sport.]

✓ [N] 3. Professional street luge racer Roger Hickey has broken more than fifty bones.
[This statement is true but *too narrow*. It tells about only one detail mentioned in the story.]

15 Score 15 points for a correct *M* answer.
10 Score 5 points for each correct *B* or *N* answer.

25 TOTAL SCORE: Finding the Main Idea

B RECALLING FACTS

How well do you remember the facts in the story you just read? Put an *x* in the box in front of the correct answer to each of the multiple-choice questions below.

1. Street luge racers can hit speeds
   - ✓ ☒ a. of sixty miles per hour or more.
   - ___ ☐ b. between forty and fifty miles per hour.
   - ___ ☐ c. of about one hundred miles per hour.

2. Street luge racers steer their boards
   - ___ ☐ a. by dragging a foot on one side at a time.
   - ___ ☐ b. by mental telepathy.
   - ✓ ☒ c. by shifting their bodies.

3. Preparations for a street luge race include
   - ___ ☐ a. removing all street signs that can be moved.
   - ✓ ☒ b. closing the street to normal traffic.
   - ___ ☐ c. installing rubber bumpers along curbs.

4. Even pros like Roger Hickey
   - ___ ☐ a. replace their brakes after each race.
   - ___ ☐ b. avoid race courses with ninety-degree turns.
   - ✓ ☒ c. face the possibility of breaking many bones.

5. One proof of street luge's popularity is that
   - ✓ ☒ a. TV sports shows have begun to cover street luge events.
   - ___ ☐ b. street luge has been around for years.
   - ___ ☐ c. those who participate love the sport.

Score 5 points for each correct answer.

_25_ TOTAL SCORE: Recalling Facts

C MAKING INFERENCES

When you use information from the text and your own experience to draw a conclusion that is not directly stated in the text, you are making an *inference*.

Below are five statements that may or may *not* be inferences based on the facts of the story. Write the letter *C* in the box in front of each statement that is a correct inference. Write the letter *F* in front of each faulty inference.

C—Correct Inference   F—Faulty Inference

- ✓ [C] 1. The way in which weight is arranged across a moving object affects the object's movement.
  [This is a *correct* inference. Paragraph 3 discusses how the racers position their bodies to steer their boards.]

- ✓ [C] 2. An early step in arranging a street luge race is notifying the local police department.
  [This is a *correct* inference. A street must be closed by local authorities before lugers may use it.]

- ✓ [F] 3. Street lugers do not spend much on gear.
  [This is a *faulty* inference. Lugers need their boards, leather clothing, helmets, special shoes, and additional padding.]

- ✓ [F] 4. Standard rules for street luge were decided on before the first races were held in the 1970s.
  [This is a *faulty* inference. At first many groups were doing street luge separately; rules were later standardized.]

- ✓ [C] 5. Street lugers will spend a great deal of time in hospitals and emergency rooms.
  [This is a *correct* inference.]

Score 5 points for each correct *C* or *F* answer.

_25_ TOTAL SCORE: Making Inferences

D USING WORDS PRECISELY

Each numbered sentence below contains an underlined word or phrase from the story you just read. Following the sentence are three definitions. One is a *synonym* for the underlined word, one is an *antonym*, and one has a completely *different* meaning than the underlined word.

For each definition, write the letter that stands for the correct answer in the box.

S—Synonym   A—Antonym   D—Different

1. They have to know exactly how to <u>position</u> their bodies when heading into a curve.

   ✓ [S] a. place

   ✓ [D] b. count

   ✓ [A] c. disarrange

2. Although they wait until these streets have been closed to traffic, many <u>hazards</u> remain.

   ✓ [A] a. items that contribute to safety

   ✓ [S] b. dangers

   ✓ [D] c. people

3. And in a bad practice run in 1995, he <u>fractured</u> his heel in three places.

   ✓ [D] a. covered

   ✓ [S] b. broke

   ✓ [A] c. mended

4. Darren Lott, author of *Street Luge Survival Guide*, writes about one young <u>daredevil</u> named Zac Bernstein.

   ✓ [S] a. a person who takes chances and acts recklessly

   ✓ [D] b. a person who plays sports for money

   ✓ [A] c. a person who is extremely careful

5. Street luge has been around for years. No one person "<u>invented</u>" it.

   ✓ [S] a. discovered

   ✓ [A] b. copied

   ✓ [D] c. interrupted

<u>15</u>   Score 3 points for a correct *S* answer.
<u>10</u>   Score 1 point for each correct *A* or *D* answer.

<u>25</u>   TOTAL SCORE: Using Words Precisely

• *Enter the total score for each exercise in the spaces below. Add the scores to find your Critical Reading Score. Then record your Critical Reading Score on the graph on page 114.*

_____	Finding the Main Idea
_____	Recalling Facts
_____	Making Inferences
_____	Using Words Precisely
_____	CRITICAL READING SCORE: Sample Unit

To the Student

Almost everybody appreciates sports of some kind. From babyhood on, you like to feel control over your movements and to increase your physical skills. In addition, sports hold other pleasures. You may enjoy the thrill of competition, the high you get from running, or the spirit of teamwork in such games as baseball and soccer. However, some athletes want yet another quality in their sports: danger. They like to know that not only are their bodies strong, but also their spirits are full of courage. The stories in *Extreme Sports* are about such people and the sports they love. Whether you agree with their attitudes or believe they are foolish thrill-seekers, you will be fascinated by their deeds.

While you are enjoying these exciting stories, you will be developing your reading skills. This book assumes that you already are a fairly good reader. *Extreme Sports* is for students who want to read faster and to increase their understanding of what they read. If you complete all fifteen units—reading the stories and completing the exercises—you will surely increase your reading rate and improve your comprehension.

Group One

Is climbing up walls of skyscrapers something that only superheroes with magic powers can do? Not according to George Willig. When he decided to climb the outside of the World Trade Center in New York City, everyone who saw him thought he was trying the impossible. Emergency workers came to "rescue" him. But as this picture shows, Willig was just out for a good time.

THE HUMAN FLY

Swimmers love to swim, dancers love to dance, and climbers . . . well, they just love to climb. If you don't believe that, ask George H. Willig. In 1977 Willig climbed the tallest thing he could find. That happened to be the World Trade Center in New York City. It was a 1,350-foot climb straight up. By the time Willig got to the top, he had earned the nickname the Human Fly.

Willig started climbing things when he was just a boy. He scrambled up trees and hillsides. In time, he moved on to mountains and cliffs. But it wasn't enough. On his twenty-sixth birthday, Willig looked around for a new challenge. That's when he thought of the World Trade Center's South Tower. It was, as he later said, a "very appealing wall. Very vertical."

Willig went to the tower and looked at its outside walls. He saw grooves designed to move window-washing equipment up and down the tower. Those grooves, he decided, were just what he needed. He could make special clamps that would lock into the grooves. The clamps would serve as grips for him. By locking and unlocking the clamps, he could move the grips—and himself—up the wall.

For almost a year, Willig worked to perfect his plan. He designed and built the clamps. He tested them in his workroom. He even went to the bottom of the tower a few times to try them out. He went at night, when no one was around. He figured that if people knew what he was planning, they would try to stop him.

At last, Willig was ready for his big climb. He arranged to take a day off from his job at a toy company. He got to the tower early on the morning of May 26, 1977. Using strong nylon rope, he tied himself to the clamps. That way, if one of his hands or feet slipped, the rope would save him. Willig knew the rope was strong enough, but he couldn't be sure about the clamps. What if they pulled out of the grooves? What if the grooves themselves split open when his weight pulled on them? Those were risks he would just have to take.

At 6:30 A.M. he started to climb. Soon a small crowd gathered to watch him. Nobody knew who he was or what he was doing. The police feared he might be trying to kill himself. They rushed a suicide expert to the scene. That worried Willig. "I was afraid the Fire Department would send a cherry picker . . . to get me," he later said. "That made me nervous and I went up as fast as I could. But once I knew I was out of the range of a cherry picker . . . I slowed down and relaxed."

In all, Willig had 110 stories to climb. By the time he reached the tenth story, people realized that he intended to go all the way. They began to cheer him on. News reporters arrived. TV stations sent camera crews. More and more people gathered in the streets. For thousands of New Yorkers, an ordinary Thursday suddenly became a special occasion.

High above them all, George Willig remained calm. "I was very much alone with myself and at peace with myself," he later said. Everything was going well. The clamps were working. The grooves were not splitting open. And so Willig just kept climbing, foot after foot after foot.

By 8:30 A.M. he was halfway to the top. There, at the fifty-fifth floor, he was met by two police officers. They had climbed out onto a platform used by window washers. They asked Willig if he was ready to quit. He said no. They asked if he wanted any help. Again he said no.

Before talking to him, the officers thought Willig was crazy. But they soon changed their minds. Clearly he was a fine climber. He knew what he was doing. "Every response he gave me was reasonable," said Officer DeWitt Allen. "The only thing unreasonable about it was the fact that he was on the outside of the building."

Allen and his partner stayed close to Willig. They promised to help him if he needed it. But he just kept moving higher. So the officers kept raising the platform. In that way, the three men moved up the building together.

By the time Willig reached the seventy-fifth floor, he was everybody's hero. Officer Allen reached out and passed him a pad of paper. He asked for Willig's autograph. Down on the street, one man looked up at Willig and asked, "What's holding him up?"

"A lot of guts," answered someone else.

At 10:05 A.M. Willig reached the roof of the tower. He had done it! He was at the top! Far below him, the crowd erupted in cheers. Drivers honked their horns. People laughed and whistled. With a smile, Willig turned and waved to his fans. One writer for the *New York Times* called it "the happiest thing that has occurred around here in many years."

There was a down side to Willig's climb, however. It turned out that what he did was not legal. A city law said no one could climb up the side of a building like that. Officer Allen and his partner had no choice. Once Willig was safely inside the tower, they had to arrest him.

The city of New York planned to fine Willig $250,000. But that angered many people. So city leaders changed their minds. They fined Willig $1.10. That was one cent for every story he had climbed. As for Willig, he was surprised by all the fuss surrounding his climb. "I just wanted the prize of climbing [the tower]," he said. "The truth is I didn't know anyone would really notice me."

If you have been timed while reading this selection, enter your reading time below. Then turn to the Words-per-Minute table on page 110 and look up your reading speed (words per minute). Enter your reading speed on the graph on page 113.

READING TIME: Unit 1
_____ : _____
Minutes   *Seconds*

12

How Well Did You Read?

- *Complete the four exercises that follow. The directions for each exercise will tell you how to mark your answers.*

- *When you have finished all four exercises, use the answer key on page 106 to check your work. For each right answer, put a check mark (✓) on the line beside the box. For each wrong answer, write the correct answer on the line.*

- *Follow the directions after each exercise to find your scores.*

A FINDING THE MAIN IDEA

A good main idea statement answers two questions: it tells *who* or *what* is the subject of the story, and it answers the understood question *does what?* or *is what?* Look at the three statements below. One expresses the main idea of the story you just read. Another statement is *too broad*; it is vague and doesn't tell much about the topic of the story. The third statement is *too narrow*; it tells about only one part of the story.

Match the statements with the three answer choices below by writing the letter of each answer in the box in front of the statement it goes with.

M—Main Idea   B—Too Broad   N—Too Narrow

_____ ☐ 1. George Willig stunned New York City with his daring climb up the wall of the World Trade Center in 1977.

_____ ☐ 2. To make his climb easier, George Willig designed special clamps to lock into grooves on the World Trade Center wall.

_____ ☐ 3. People who love to climb will usually find something to climb wherever they are.

_____ Score 15 points for a correct *M* answer.
_____ Score 5 points for each correct *B* or *N* answer.

_____ TOTAL SCORE: Finding the Main Idea

RECALLING FACTS

How well do you remember the facts in the story you just read? Put an *x* in the box in front of the correct answer to each of the multiple-choice questions below.

1. The grooves in the World Trade Center wall were designed to
   ___ ☐ a. carry rain water down the wall.
   ___ ☐ b. move window-washing equipment up and down.
   ___ ☐ c. make the bare wall more appealing.

2. Willig planned to climb the World Trade Center
   ___ ☐ a. for almost a year.
   ___ ☐ b. for a few weeks.
   ___ ☐ c. since his childhood.

3. At first, police thought that Willig was
   ___ ☐ a. lost.
   ___ ☐ b. a terrorist trying to bomb the tower.
   ___ ☐ c. trying to kill himself.

4. When Willig reached the top of the building,
   ___ ☐ a. the police arrested him.
   ___ ☐ b. he threw his equipment over the side.
   ___ ☐ c. he decided to become a window washer.

5. The city of New York fined Willig a total of
   ___ ☐ a. $1.10.
   ___ ☐ b. $1,000.
   ___ ☐ c. $250,000.

Score 5 points for each correct answer.

___ TOTAL SCORE: Recalling Facts

MAKING INFERENCES

When you use information from the text and your own experience to draw a conclusion that is not directly stated in the text, you are making an *inference*.

Below are five statements that may or may *not* be inferences based on the facts of the story. Write the letter *C* in the box in front of each statement that is a correct inference. Write the letter *F* in front of each faulty inference.

C—Correct Inference   F—Faulty Inference

___ ☐ 1. Willig knew that there was a chance that the climb he was planning would not be welcomed by everyone.

___ ☐ 2. Willig was a creative, inventive, and careful planner.

___ ☐ 3. The Fire Department's cherry picker could extend up to the top of the World Trade Center.

___ ☐ 4. Even busy city people can be excited by an act of skill and bravery.

___ ☐ 5. The fine that Willig paid to the city of New York will most likely discourage other people from climbing the World Trade Center.

Score 5 points for each correct *C* or *F* answer.

___ TOTAL SCORE: Making Inferences

D USING WORDS PRECISELY

Each numbered sentence below contains an underlined word or phrase from the story you just read. Following the sentence are three definitions. One is a *synonym* for the underlined word, one is an *antonym*, and one has a completely *different* meaning than the underlined word.

For each definition, write the letter that stands for the correct answer in the box.

S—Synonym   A—Antonym   D—Different

1. He <u>scrambled</u> up trees and hillsides.

____ ☐ a. walked slowly

____ ☐ b. moved quickly, especially on hands and knees

____ ☐ c. flew

2. It was, as he later said, a "very appealing wall. Very <u>vertical</u>."

____ ☐ a. straight up and down

____ ☐ b. inviting

____ ☐ c. straight side to side

3. By the time he reached the tenth story, people realized that he <u>intended</u> to go all the way.

____ ☐ a. did not want

____ ☐ b. climbed

____ ☐ c. planned

4. Every response he gave me was <u>reasonable</u>.

____ ☐ a. sensible

____ ☐ b. silly

____ ☐ c. colorful

5. Down on the street, one man looked up at Willig and asked, "What's holding him up?"
"A lot of <u>guts</u>," answered someone else.

____ ☐ a. equipment

____ ☐ b. cowardice

____ ☐ c. courage

____ Score 3 points for a correct *S* answer.
____ Score 1 point for each correct *A* or *D* answer.

____ TOTAL SCORE: Using Words Precisely

• *Enter the total score for each exercise in the spaces below. Add the scores to find your Critical Reading Score. Then record your Critical Reading Score on the graph on page 114.*

____ Finding the Main Idea
____ Recalling Facts
____ Making Inferences
____ Using Words Precisely

____ CRITICAL READING SCORE: Unit 1

Look out below! From this bungee jumper's point of view, humans on the ground below are as tiny as ants. Bungee jumpers regularly enjoy free falls of 150 feet before their bungee cords pull them back to avoid violent collisions with the earth.

BUNGEE JUMPING: A LEAP OF FAITH

Anyone can do it. But it helps to be a little crazy. The idea is simple enough. You climb a high tower or crane. Or perhaps you go up in a hot-air balloon. In any case, someone attaches a thick rubber band around your ankles. Then you leap out into the wild blue yonder. Your body plunges toward the earth below. Then, at the last moment, the rubber band stops you. This is not your day to die.

The sport is called bungee jumping. It began long ago as a ritual on certain islands in the South Pacific. (These islands form the present-day country of Vanuatu.) Each spring the islanders gathered vines. They wove them into a kind of rope. Then young men called "land divers" climbed high towers. They tied the vines to their ankles and jumped. They did it to prove their courage. A good jump was also supposed to help ensure healthy crops for the island.

Modern bungee jumping began in England on April 1, 1979. Note the day. It was April *Fool's* Day. The members of the Oxford Dangerous Sports Club were looking for a new thrill. They had heard of "land diving"

and wanted to try it for themselves. So the men climbed up a high bridge, tied rubber cords to their ankles, and jumped. One member later said the jump was "quite pleasurable, really."

But it was a man from New Zealand who made bungee jumping a big sport. His name was Alan John Hackett. Hackett was quite a daredevil. He had once jumped off the Eiffel Tower in Paris, France. Now, in 1988, he wanted to give others a chance to try bungee jumping. At this time, though, the sport was illegal. So Hackett made a deal with New Zealand police. Using his own money, he would fix up a dilapidated bridge over a river gorge. In return, the police let him open a legal bungee jumping center on the bridge.

The center was a huge success. Hackett gave each jumper a special T-shirt. It became a hot item among daredevils. Everyone wanted one of those shirts. And since the only way to get one was to make a jump, more and more people agreed to do it. Some jumpers did really wild things. They asked to jump with an extralong cord. That way they would dip into the

river before the cord pulled them back. One man put shampoo on his head. When he bounced up out of the water, he was washing his hair!

Bungee jumping soon caught on in the United States. It was introduced in California and Colorado. Then it spread to other states. At first, only the boldest people did it. But over time, others joined in. All kinds of people took the plunge. Even one man who was helped out of a wheelchair jumped. And no jumpers complained about paying $50 or more to do it.

As thrills go, it's hard to beat bungee jumping. The platforms used for the jumps are ten stories high—or higher. That means jumpers fall as far as 150 feet before the cord saves them. First-time jumpers can almost taste their fear. Jay Petrow thought about it for a year before he jumped. He said his palms began to sweat just thinking about it. Emily Trask said, "The first time I jumped, I was terrified." Nora Jacobson said, "My terror [was] cold and rippling."

Some jumpers use humor to calm their nerves. Just before her first jump,

Bungee cords may be attached to jumpers' waists or ankles. This daredevil, like early Vanuatu jumpers, uses the ankle cord.

a woman named Alison was asked how old she was. "I hope to be twenty-nine soon," she replied. Most jumpers are young, but some are not. S. L. Potter made his first leap at the age of one hundred. "It was now or never," he later explained.

There is, of course, real danger. There is no margin for error in bungee jumping. One mistake, and you're history. And while most people live to tell the tale, a few don't. In 1989 two French jumpers died when their cords broke. A third died when he slammed into a tower. In 1991 Hal Irish became the first American jumper to die. Somehow his cord became detached as he dove through the air.

So accidents *do* happen. But for many, the danger just adds to the excitement. Besides, bungee jumpers don't talk about the tragedies. They talk about the triumphs. They talk about facing their fears. And they talk about the joy of the fall itself. During a jump, a person hits speeds of sixty miles an hour. Then, when the cord tightens, the jumper springs back up into the air like a rocket. For a short time, he or she is a kind of human yo-yo, bouncing up and down in the breeze. When the cord loses its bounce, the ride is over.

Even then, though, some of the joy remains. Jumpers feel both happy and relieved when it's over. Most laugh and smile as they are unhooked from the cord. "Hey, look at me! I did it!" many of them shout. It is, as one person said, "a natural high." Bungee jumpers even have a name for this soaring feeling. They call it the post-bungee grin. Maybe someday you'll decide to make that leap of faith and share that grin. All it takes is a little money—and a lot of nerve.

If you have been timed while reading this selection, enter your reading time below. Then turn to the Words-per-Minute table on page 110 and look up your reading speed (words per minute). Enter your reading speed on the graph on page 113.

<table>
<tr><td colspan="2">READING TIME: Unit 2</td></tr>
<tr><td>_____</td><td>: _____</td></tr>
<tr><td>Minutes</td><td>Seconds</td></tr>
</table>

How Well Did You Read?

- *Complete the four exercises that follow. The directions for each exercise will tell you how to mark your answers.*

- *When you have finished all four exercises, use the answer key on page 106 to check your work. For each right answer, put a check mark (✓) on the line beside the box. For each wrong answer, write the correct answer on the line.*

- *Follow the directions after each exercise to find your scores.*

A FINDING THE MAIN IDEA

A good main idea statement answers two questions: it tells *who* or *what* is the subject of the story, and it answers the understood question *does what?* or *is what?* Look at the three statements below. One expresses the main idea of the story you just read. Another statement is *too broad*; it is vague and doesn't tell much about the topic of the story. The third statement is *too narrow*; it tells about only one part of the story.

Match the statements with the three answer choices below by writing the letter of each answer in the box in front of the statement it goes with.

M—Main Idea   **B—Too Broad**   **N—Too Narrow**

_____ ☐ 1. Thousands of bungee jumpers have leaped from heights at the end of a strong rubber band both to enjoy flying through the air and to prove courage.

_____ ☐ 2. Of the thousands of people who have done bungee jumping, perhaps the oldest is S. L. Potter, who made his first leap at the age of one hundred.

_____ ☐ 3. Although it is based on a long-standing tradition in certain South Pacific islands, bungee jumping has acquired worldwide popularity only recently.

_____ Score 15 points for a correct *M* answer.
_____ Score 5 points for each correct *B* or *N* answer.

_____ TOTAL SCORE: Finding the Main Idea

B RECALLING FACTS

How well do you remember the facts in the story you just read? Put an *x* in the box in front of the correct answer to each of the multiple-choice questions below.

1. "Land divers" in Vanuatu depended on
   - ☐ a. thick rubber bands tied to their ankles.
   - ☐ b. cords made of vines tied to their ankles.
   - ☐ c. ropes made of leather tied to their ankles.

2. Members of the Oxford Dangerous Sports Club
   - ☐ a. made their famous dive in Vanuatu.
   - ☐ b. jumped from London Bridge.
   - ☐ c. started bungee jumping on April 1, 1979.

3. Bungee promoter Alan John Hackett was from
   - ☐ a. New Zealand.
   - ☐ b. California.
   - ☐ c. England.

4. To get Hackett's special T-shirts, people jumped
   - ☐ a. off a bridge.
   - ☐ b. off the Eiffel Tower.
   - ☐ c. out of a hot-air balloon.

5. The term *post-bungee grin* refers to the
   - ☐ a. smile with which bungee jumpers recall long-past jumps.
   - ☐ b. happy face on Hackett's T-shirts.
   - ☐ c. feeling of joy and pride one feels immediately after bungee jumping.

Score 5 points for each correct answer.

_____ TOTAL SCORE: Recalling Facts

C MAKING INFERENCES

When you use information from the text and your own experience to draw a conclusion that is not directly stated in the text, you are making an *inference*.

Below are five statements that may or may *not* be inferences based on the facts of the story. Write the letter *C* in the box in front of each statement that is a correct inference. Write the letter *F* in front of each faulty inference.

C—Correct Inference   F—Faulty Inference

1. The people of Vanuatu would think bungee jumpers are courageous.

2. In 1979 members of the Oxford Dangerous Sports Club were sure that bungee jumping would become a popular sport within a short time.

3. Before 1988 New Zealand authorities considered bungee jumping a threat to public safety.

4. Bungee jumping requires that the jumper have a great deal of physical strength.

5. Bungee jumping is clearly more dangerous than riding a motorcycle without a helmet.

Score 5 points for each correct *C* or *F* answer.

_____ TOTAL SCORE: Making Inferences

D USING WORDS PRECISELY

Each numbered sentence below contains an underlined word or phrase from the story you just read. Following the sentence are three definitions. One is a *synonym* for the underlined word, one is an *antonym*, and one has a completely *different* meaning than the underlined word.

For each definition, write the letter that stands for the correct answer in the box.

S—Synonym   A—Antonym   D—Different

1. It began long ago as a <u>ritual</u> on certain islands in the South Pacific.

____ ☐ a. celebration

____ ☐ b. formal, traditional event

____ ☐ c. unplanned, disorganized event

2. A good jump was also supposed to help <u>ensure</u> healthy crops for the island.

____ ☐ a. guarantee

____ ☐ b. make well known

____ ☐ c. reduce the chances of

3. One member later said the jump was "quite <u>pleasurable</u>, really."

____ ☐ a. fast-moving

____ ☐ b. unpleasant

____ ☐ c. enjoyable

4. Now, in 1988, he wanted to give others a chance to try bungee jumping. At this time, though, the sport was <u>illegal</u>.

____ ☐ a. lawful

____ ☐ b. not understood

____ ☐ c. against the law

5. Using his own money, he would fix up a <u>dilapidated</u> bridge over a river gorge.

____ ☐ a. shabby

____ ☐ b. new and attractive

____ ☐ c. out-of-the-way

____ Score 3 points for a correct *S* answer.
____ Score 1 point for each correct *A* or *D* answer.

____ TOTAL SCORE: Using Words Precisely

• *Enter the total score for each exercise in the spaces below. Add the scores to find your Critical Reading Score. Then record your Critical Reading Score on the graph on page 114.*

_____ Finding the Main Idea
_____ Recalling Facts
_____ Making Inferences
_____ Using Words Precisely

_____ CRITICAL READING SCORE: Unit 2

White foam shooting up out of swirling waters all around you . . . beyond the water, high cliffs rising at both sides . . . jagged rocks jutting up out of the water . . . and pressing in on you, the roar of the rapids and rushing wind—you are white water rafting!

WHITE WATER THRILLS

You can go to Disney World and ride Splash Mountain. It's safe and lots of fun. But Splash Mountain is the same ride over and over again. If you want to try something different, try white water rafting. A white water ride is never the same twice. New thrills and dangers lie downstream every time you "run the rapids."

"White water" means river rapids. The water becomes a foamy "white" when it swirls over and around rocks. All rapids are called white water. But not all white water rivers are the same. Some are pretty tame; others are really wild. Rafters need to know what they are facing. A gentle-looking river can turn into a beast around the next bend. So all rivers are rated based on how hard they are to travel down.

The most common rating system uses Roman numerals from I to VI. A Class I river is wide with a few small waves. It's not much more exciting than a splash in an old bathtub. A Class III river is much more difficult. It has rocks and waves up to three feet high. You can expect to get wet running the rapids of a Class III river.

If you move up to a Class V river, you will face violent rapids with no breaks. You can get killed on a Class V river. A Class VI river is even worse. It's a real hair-raiser. All kinds of dangers await you there. Anyone who takes on a Class VI river must be two things—an expert and a daredevil. A few rivers have sections that are off the scale. These "Class VII" rivers can't be rafted by anyone.

Rivers change all the time. A heavy rain can turn a Class III river into a Class V or even a Class VI. Some rivers can be run only in the spring after the snow melts. The rest of the time there just isn't enough water in them.

Rivers are like magnets for thrill seekers. Some people run the rapids in canoes. Others use one-person kayaks. Still others choose sixteen-foot rubber rafts. The rafts have one big advantage. They can stay afloat on rivers that would swamp a canoe or kayak.

One of the top ten white water rivers in the world is the Gauley River. It runs through West Virginia. The Gauley is a rafter's dream . . . or—if you're not careful—a nightmare. It has twenty-eight miles of heart-pounding rapids. Each set of rapids has its own name. Some give fair warning to rafters. One is called Pure Screaming Hell. There are also Lost Paddle, Heaven Help Us, and Pillow Rock. River guide Roger Harrison describes Pillow Rock this way: "[It's] fifteen seconds of uncontrolled violence."

Clearly, white water rafting is not for the meek. Dangers lurk everywhere. There is, for example, something called a "keeper." A keeper is a kind of whirlpool. It is created when water rushes over a huge rock with a steep face. A keeper has enough water power to trap, or keep, a boat for days. Imagine what it could do to a person! Keepers cause more drownings than any other hazard.

There are other pitfalls as well. There are waterfalls, fallen tree limbs, and sharp boulders. Any one of these can spell disaster. And no rafter wants to be caught in a "Colorado sandwich." That can happen when a raft hits a big wave. The front and back of the raft are folded up toward the center. Anyone in the middle is lunch meat in a raft sandwich.

Most rafters know the risks. And they are willing to take them. But they also do what they can to cut down the dangers. They carry at least fifty feet of strong rope for towing. They often wear wet suits and life jackets in case they get flipped into the water. And they wear helmets in case they hit a rock when they're dumped overboard.

Rafters also wear waterproof shoes. Some rookies want to take their shoes off as soon as they get wet. Wet shoes are uncomfortable. And rookies worry that wearing shoes will make it harder to swim if they're dumped into the water. But taking off their shoes would be a mistake. Shoes offer rafters' feet their only protection from rocks.

Look at it this way: if you end up in the river, you can't swim anyway. The current is just too strong. All you can do is float on your back with your feet pointed down the river. You'll need your feet to help steer around the rocks. If you're wearing shoes, your feet won't get cut up too badly. And when you finally reach the shore, you'll be glad you're wearing shoes. It might be a long walk home over very rocky ground!

Every year, thousands of people enjoy white water rafting. But once in a while, the sport turns deadly. That happened in the summer of 1987. There were four accidents in British Columbia. Twelve rafters died in the span of eight weeks. The rivers in that part of Canada are snow-fed. They are very cold. Five of the dead rafters were American businessmen looking for a thrill. On August 1, they took on the wild Chilko River without wet suits. A huge wave knocked them out of their raft. The men died in the frigid water.

So to enjoy the sport, you *must* respect the power of the river. That means playing it as safe as possible. But no extreme sport is completely safe. Dave Arnold owns a rafting company on the Gauley River. He warns his customers about the potential risks. Arnold and his guides are cautious. They make sure people know what they are doing. As Arnold puts it, "We never say rafting is safe."

If you have been timed while reading this selection, enter your reading time below. Then turn to the Words-per-Minute table on page 110 and look up your reading speed (words per minute). Enter your reading speed on the graph on page 113.

READING TIME: Unit 3	
_____ : _____	
Minutes	*Seconds*

How Well Did You Read?

- *Complete the four exercises that follow. The directions for each exercise will tell you how to mark your answers.*

- *When you have finished all four exercises, use the answer key on page 106 to check your work. For each right answer, put a check mark (✓) on the line beside the box. For each wrong answer, write the correct answer on the line.*

- *Follow the directions after each exercise to find your scores.*

A FINDING THE MAIN IDEA

A good main idea statement answers two questions: it tells *who* or *what* is the subject of the story, and it answers the understood question *does what?* or *is what?* Look at the three statements below. One expresses the main idea of the story you just read. Another statement is *too broad*; it is vague and doesn't tell much about the topic of the story. The third statement is *too narrow*; it tells about only one part of the story.

Match the statements with the three answer choices below by writing the letter of each answer in the box in front of the statement it goes with.

M—Main Idea   **B—Too Broad**   **N—Too Narrow**

____ ☐ 1. Rivers are rated using Roman numerals from I to VI, depending on how hard they are to travel down.

____ ☐ 2. White water rafting is a sport that offers excitement and thrills.

____ ☐ 3. While it offers fun and excitement, white water rafting requires careful planning and an awareness of its risks.

____ Score 15 points for a correct *M* answer.
____ Score 5 points for each correct *B* or *N* answer.

____ TOTAL SCORE: Finding the Main Idea

B RECALLING FACTS

How well do you remember the facts in the story you just read? Put an *x* in the box in front of the correct answer to each of the multiple-choice questions below.

1. A Class I river
   - ☐ a. has rocks and waves up to three feet high.
   - ☐ b. has violent rapids with no breaks.
   - ☐ c. is wide with a few small waves.

2. A Class III river can turn into a Class V river if
   - ☐ a. a heavy rain falls.
   - ☐ b. no rain falls for weeks.
   - ☐ c. you are not an experienced rafter.

3. One danger, known as a "keeper," is a
   - ☐ a. whirlpool that holds a boat underwater.
   - ☐ b. big wave that can sink a raft.
   - ☐ c. fallen tree limb that can put a hole in a raft.

4. It's a good idea to wear shoes in a raft because
   - ☐ a. your feet get uncomfortable if they get wet.
   - ☐ b. wearing shoes helps you steer the raft.
   - ☐ c. shoes will protect your feet from rocks if you end up in the river.

5. Some rivers in British Columbia are dangerously cold because they are
   - ☐ a. so far north.
   - ☐ b. fed by melting snow.
   - ☐ c. very deep.

Score 5 points for each correct answer.

_____ TOTAL SCORE: Recalling Facts

C MAKING INFERENCES

When you use information from the text and your own experience to draw a conclusion that is not directly stated in the text, you are making an *inference*.

Below are five statements that may or may *not* be inferences based on the facts of the story. Write the letter *C* in the box in front of each statement that is a correct inference. Write the letter *F* in front of each faulty inference.

C—Correct Inference   F—Faulty Inference

_____ ☐ 1. Wet suits keep swimmers in cold water much warmer than ordinary clothing does.

_____ ☐ 2. You would be foolish to attempt to raft a Class VII river.

_____ ☐ 3. It would be wise to run the Gauley River in a canoe rather than a raft.

_____ ☐ 4. If you take a camera down the river, you should make sure that it is waterproof.

_____ ☐ 5. The dangers of white water rafting make it an unpopular sport with almost everyone.

Score 5 points for each correct *C* or *F* answer.

_____ TOTAL SCORE: Making Inferences

D USING WORDS PRECISELY

Each numbered sentence below contains an underlined word or phrase from the story you just read. Following the sentence are three definitions. One is a *synonym* for the underlined word, one is an *antonym*, and one has a completely *different* meaning than the underlined word.

For each definition, write the letter that stands for the correct answer in the box.

S—Synonym   A—Antonym   D—Different

1. Some <u>rookies</u> want to take their shoes off as soon as they get wet.

____ ☐ a. rafters

____ ☐ b. beginners

____ ☐ c. people with experience

2. They can stay afloat on rivers that would <u>swamp</u> a canoe or kayak.

____ ☐ a. dry out

____ ☐ b. light

____ ☐ c. fill with water

3. Clearly, white water rafting is not for the <u>meek</u>.

____ ☐ a. timid

____ ☐ b. bold and daring

____ ☐ c. elderly

4. There are other <u>pitfalls</u> as well. There are waterfalls, fallen tree limbs, and sharp boulders.

____ ☐ a. sights

____ ☐ b. benefits

____ ☐ c. hidden dangers

5. He warns his customers about the <u>potential</u> risks.

____ ☐ a. likely

____ ☐ b. many

____ ☐ c. impossible

____ Score 3 points for a correct *S* answer.
____ Score 1 point for each correct *A* or *D* answer.

____ TOTAL SCORE: Using Words Precisely

• *Enter the total score for each exercise in the spaces below. Add the scores to find your Critical Reading Score. Then record your Critical Reading Score on the graph on page 114.*

____ Finding the Main Idea
____ Recalling Facts
____ Making Inferences
____ Using Words Precisely

____ CRITICAL READING SCORE: Unit 3

Did you ever imagine yourself floating on the breeze? You may want to try hang gliding. One pilot described the experience this way: "You really feel like a bird. You feel the wind on you and the flutter of the sail." Here, a pilot glides over the ocean in an evening flight.

HANG GLIDING: RIDING THE WIND

It all started one day back in the 1960s. Water-skier Bill Moyes tied a long kite to the back of a motorboat. He attached himself to the kite with a harness. Then he motioned for the motorboat to take off. Moments later, the speeding boat pulled the kite—and Moyes—high up into the air.

It was a great ride. Moyes looked down at the sparkling water far below. He soared soundlessly through the air, feeling almost like a bird. The plan was for the boat driver to slow the boat down gradually. That would cause Moyes to sink back to earth. But all at once, Moyes spotted trouble ahead. The motorboat was pulling him right toward some high-tension wires! At that point Moyes did the only thing he could think of: he released the rope that tied him to the boat.

Suddenly, Moyes truly was flying like a bird. He was no longer connected to anything on the ground. The wings of the kite kept him from plummeting. They caught the wind and allowed him to glide gently down to earth. And so he completed the world's first hang gliding journey.

From then on, Moyes was hooked. He made lots of flights with his "wings" strapped on. He stopped using a motorboat to get into the air. Instead, he just climbed to the top of a ledge or cliff and jumped off. In 1970 he even soared over the Grand Canyon. Others began following his lead. Like Moyes, they used kites with flexible wings. They also figured out how to steer by shifting their weight back and forth.

When hang gliding "pilots" take off, they may plunge through the air in a free fall for ten or twenty feet. Then their wings catch air currents and they begin to rise. By gliding from current to current, hang gliding pilots can float among the clouds for hours. They can make their gliders do loops, dives, and turns. And they can land with pinpoint accuracy.

These pilots make it look easy. And in some ways, it is. There's no motor to worry about. There are no complicated instruments. It's just you, your wings, and the wind. It is, says one pilot, "the closest approach man has to pure flight."

But hang gliding has a darker side. It can be dangerous. In fact, it can be downright deadly. More than one pilot has died while trying to navigate a glider. Many others have been badly hurt. In 1993, twenty-nine-year-old Leonard Stabb went hang gliding in the mountains of New York. There was very little wind that day. So Stabb decided to add some excitement to his flight. He steered his glider near some trees, but he got too close. He smashed into a tree. He was so badly injured that doctors were not sure he would live. Stabb did live, but he never fully recovered from the accident.

Bob Abbott was even less fortunate. He was hang gliding in New Mexico in 1981. For a while, he sailed smoothly through the air. Then winds began to carry him toward some storm clouds. Abbott found his peaceful ride becoming rockier. Soon he found himself in the middle of a thunderstorm. He tried to fight his way through it. But the storm was too intense. The glider crashed. The twenty-six-year-old Abbott did not survive.

Clearly, thunderstorms and trees are big dangers. But there are others as well. Pilots must be careful not to take off in winds that are too high. They have to be especially careful to avoid "rotors." Those are strong winds that come rolling in off mountains. Rotors can cut through a regular wind current and send the glider spinning out of control. They can cause a glider to take a nosedive straight down. That's called "going over the falls."

Sometimes, when pilots go over the falls, they can steady the glider and bring it safely out of the dive. But sometimes they can't. Then even the best pilots have to bail out. In the 1993 World Hang Gliding Championships, top pilot Brad Koji went over the falls. As he did so, his body slammed into the wings of his glider. Luckily, Koji was wearing a parachute. He was able to open his chute and float fourteen thousand feet back to earth.

Pilots also have to be on the lookout for "dust devils." These are tight swirls of air that lift sand, dirt, and bits of litter off the ground. They can also lift up a glider. Italian pilot Andrea Noseda was caught in a dust devil in 1993. Noseda's glider was pulled up into the air then smashed back to the ground. Noseda broke three bones in the crash.

At times, pilots seem to be asking for trouble. They pick takeoff points that add to the risks. For instance, some hang gliding pilots jump off from Dead Horse Point. That is a two-thousand-foot sandstone cliff in Utah. At the bottom of the cliff lie a cactus or two—and a whole bunch of jagged rocks. As one man put it, "If you make a mistake going off this cliff, you're dead." When Reggie Jones peered over Dead Horse Point for the first time, he felt his stomach turn to knots. "I can't do it," he blurted out. "I can't jump."

Jones did jump, but he is not the only one to have felt that kind of terror. Many people have struggled to control their panic just before takeoff. As one pilot put it, "It's the fear. It's most intense before you launch. Then it's okay."

In fact, once you're in the air, the ride is much more than simply "okay." It is fantastic. Pilots say they feel great joy as they soar high above the earth. Dave Kilbourne put it this way: "You're out in the open with nothing around you; sometimes you forget you even have a kite." Said Karen Rowley, "You really feel like a bird. You feel the wind on you and the flutter of the sail. It really is like you're a part of [the glider itself]." It is that thrill—the thrill of flying free—that makes hang gliding so appealing. Many pilots feel a special bond with the birds they meet in the sky. Reggie Jones knows that feeling. "I used to be a duck hunter," he said. "But ever since I started gliding, I haven't been able to kill a bird."

If you have been timed while reading this selection, enter your reading time below. Then turn to the Words-per-Minute table on page 110 and look up your reading speed (words per minute). Enter your reading speed on the graph on page 113.

READING TIME: Unit 4	
_____ : _____	
Minutes	*Seconds*

How Well Did You Read?

- *Complete the four exercises that follow. The directions for each exercise will tell you how to mark your answers.*

- *When you have finished all four exercises, use the answer key on page 106 to check your work. For each right answer, put a check mark (✓) on the line beside the box. For each wrong answer, write the correct answer on the line.*

- *Follow the directions after each exercise to find your scores.*

 FINDING THE MAIN IDEA

A good main idea statement answers two questions: it tells *who* or *what* is the subject of the story, and it answers the understood question *does what?* or *is what?* Look at the three statements below. One expresses the main idea of the story you just read. Another statement is *too broad*; it is vague and doesn't tell much about the topic of the story. The third statement is *too narrow*; it tells about only one part of the story.

Match the statements with the three answer choices below by writing the letter of each answer in the box in front of the statement it goes with.

M—Main Idea   B—Too Broad   N—Too Narrow

_____ ☐ 1. Strong winds can spell disaster for hang gliders, as one rider discovered when he was carried into a thunderstorm.

_____ ☐ 2. Hang gliding requires skill as well as the proper equipment.

_____ ☐ 3. Hang gliders, who float through the air attached to kites with wings, come as close to flying like birds as human beings can.

_____ Score 15 points for a correct *M* answer.
_____ Score 5 points for each correct *B* or *N* answer.

_____ TOTAL SCORE: Finding the Main Idea

B RECALLING FACTS

How well do you remember the facts in the story you just read? Put an *x* in the box in front of the correct answer to each of the multiple-choice questions below.

1. The first time he hang glided, Bill Moyes released the tow rope so he could avoid
   - ☐ a. high-tension wires.
   - ☐ b. a large ship coming his way.
   - ☐ c. another water-skier.

2. Kite wings are important because they
   - ☐ a. protect the pilot from rain and wind.
   - ☐ b. remind the pilot of birds' wings.
   - ☐ c. catch air currents and lift the kite.

3. Pilots must watch out for "rotors," which are
   - ☐ a. nearby airplanes.
   - ☐ b. strong winds that roll off mountains.
   - ☐ c. radio and TV antennae.

4. When pilots "go over the falls," it means that they
   - ☐ a. fall rapidly.
   - ☐ b. fly into a body of water.
   - ☐ c. give up hang gliding.

5. Reggie Jones doesn't hunt ducks anymore because he
   - ☐ a. is afraid that someday he will mistake a hang glider for a duck and will shoot its pilot.
   - ☐ b. feels a special bond with birds now.
   - ☐ c. wants to observe ducks flying.

Score 5 points for each correct answer.

____ TOTAL SCORE: Recalling Facts

C MAKING INFERENCES

When you use information from the text and your own experience to draw a conclusion that is not directly stated in the text, you are making an *inference*.

Below are five statements that may or may *not* be inferences based on the facts of the story. Write the letter C in the box in front of each statement that is a correct inference. Write the letter F in front of each faulty inference.

C—Correct Inference   F—Faulty Inference

1. Hang glider pilots should check the weather forecast before they take off.

2. Unlike airplane flying, hang gliding is always done within a few hundred feet of the earth.

3. People who hang glide are the only athletes to feel frightened before they participate in their sport.

4. Bill Moyes had not been at all interested in sports before he started hang gliding.

5. Hang glider pilots have less control of their vehicles than airplane pilots have of theirs.

Score 5 points for each correct C or F answer.

____ TOTAL SCORE: Making Inferences

D USING WORDS PRECISELY

Each numbered sentence below contains an underlined word or phrase from the story you just read. Following the sentence are three definitions. One is a *synonym* for the underlined word, one is an *antonym*, and one has a completely *different* meaning than the underlined word.

For each definition, write the letter that stands for the correct answer in the box.

S—Synonym   A—Antonym   D—Different

1. The plan was for the boat driver to slow the boat down <u>gradually</u>.

___ ☐ a. a little at a time

___ ☐ b. all at once

___ ☐ c. kindly

2. The wings of the kite kept him from <u>plummeting</u>.

___ ☐ a. carrying

___ ☐ b. falling suddenly

___ ☐ c. rising slowly

3. Like Moyes, they used kites with <u>flexible</u> wings.

___ ☐ a. bendable

___ ☐ b. plastic

___ ☐ c. stiff

4. There are no <u>complicated</u> instruments.

___ ☐ a. favorite

___ ☐ b. simple

___ ☐ c. difficult to understand

5. More than one pilot has died while trying to <u>navigate</u> a glider.

___ ☐ a. move without a set direction

___ ☐ b. land

___ ☐ c. steer

___ Score 3 points for a correct *S* answer.
___ Score 1 point for each correct *A* or *D* answer.

___ TOTAL SCORE: Using Words Precisely

• *Enter the total score for each exercise in the spaces below. Add the scores to find your Critical Reading Score. Then record your Critical Reading Score on the graph on page 114.*

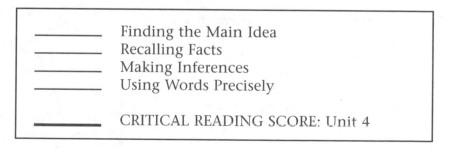

_____ Finding the Main Idea
_____ Recalling Facts
_____ Making Inferences
_____ Using Words Precisely

_____ CRITICAL READING SCORE: Unit 4

Climbing a steep slope is hard enough at sea level. But five and a half miles up, it's much harder. The air is thin, the wind is biting, and deep snow hides dangers. In addition, hardy mountain climbers must carry heavy loads. But for some, this is the only way to live.

CLIMBING THE WORLD'S HIGHEST MOUNTAINS

Death is everywhere in these mountains. It lurks behind every gust of wind. It hides under every crack in the snow. Dozens of people have died here in the mountains of Asia. Yet climbers keep coming back. They come from around the world to take on peaks such as K2 and Everest.

Climbing small mountains is hard enough. You need strong ropes, special boots, and lots of courage. But climbing the world's highest mountains is even tougher. The higher you go, the thinner the air gets. By the time you reach 20,000 feet, your body can hardly function. There is barely enough oxygen in the air to keep you alive.

Most climbers carry small tanks of oxygen. But these tanks don't hold much. So parts of the climb must be done on your own. As your brain becomes starved for oxygen, you may find yourself getting dizzy and confused. Your nose might start to bleed. You might feel sick to your stomach. This altitude sickness is no joke. In 1993 a climber on K2 died from it.

Others, too, have struggled in the thin air. One was Andrzej Zawada. Zawada was a well-known climber. He had worked his way up many tall mountains. In 1980 he led a group up Mount Everest. At 29,028 feet, it is the highest peak in the world. The climb was a success. But it wasn't easy. "I felt the lack of oxygen very much," Zawada wrote.

Zawada's group also had to deal with bad weather. That is a classic problem on these mountains. Temperatures often drop far below zero. Zawada's men were hit by bitterly cold air. At one point, it was forty degrees below zero *inside their tent*!

Sometimes things warm up a bit. Even so, blizzards can move in quickly. K2, the world's second highest mountain, is famous for its storms. They can last for days. They can bury climbers in several feet of new snow. In 1986, five people died when they were trapped in this kind of storm on K2.

Each snowfall brings yet another hazard. The weight of new snow can cause an avalanche. If you're caught

in an avalanche on Everest or one of the other big mountains, there's not much you can do. Just the thought of being caught in an avalanche makes climbers shiver with fear.

Scott Fischer almost died that way. In 1992 he and Ed Viesturs were climbing K2. Suddenly, huge chunks of snow crashed down on them. Fischer was swept down the mountain. Viesturs, who was roped to him, also began to fall. Luckily, Viesturs managed to dig his ice ax into the ground. The two men came to a stop at the edge of a 4,000-foot cliff.

Winds also pose a threat. They may whip past at one hundred miles per hour. In 1995 Alison Hargreaves fell victim to these winds. Hargreaves was one of the best climbers in the world. She was the first woman ever to reach the top of Mount Everest alone and without an oxygen tank. Only one other person had ever done this before.

On August 13, 1995, Hargreaves was on K2. Winds were high. Late that day, she and five other climbers struggled to the top of the mountain. They started back down again. But the winds grew worse, slowing the group's progress. All night, fierce gusts swirled around the mountain. Hargreaves and the others kept going. They tried to get back to their campsite. But they never made it. It appears that sometime during this frightful night, they were swept off their feet. They were literally blown to their deaths. Hargreaves's body was later found in an icy nook not far from camp.

And then there is the danger of falling into a crevasse. A crevasse is a narrow crack in the ice. It may be hundreds of feet deep. If there is a little fresh snow covering it, you may not see it until it's too late. Scott Fischer once fell into a crevasse. He didn't fall far, but his body became jammed in the crack. He was locked between two walls of ice. When another climber pulled him out, Fischer found that his right arm had been twisted out of its socket.

The list of dangers goes on and on. Mountain climbers can be blinded by the glare of sunlight reflecting off the snow. That happened to Peggy Luce. The year was 1988. Luce was trying to become the second American woman ever to reach the top of Mount Everest. Her goggles became foggy on the way up. She took them off and kept climbing. Luce made it to the top. But as she came back down, she had trouble seeing. She realized she was suffering from snow blindness. People usually recover from this, but it takes a while. Luce knew she had to keep going. She had to get out of the sun and rest her eyes. She stumbled on down the mountain. At one point, she bent over to see where she was putting her foot. She lost her balance. She began to roll down the mountain. Luckily, she dug her ice ax into the snow, stopping her fall. Luce made it to safety. But the next day, her eyes were swollen shut.

Sometimes climbers simply run out of energy. Then they might collapse in the snow and wait for death to come. Perhaps that's what happened to a German woman who died on Everest in the 1970s. She was later found, frozen in a sitting position with her head on her knees. "She made it to the top, but she didn't get down," concluded climber David Breashears.

Given all the hardships, why do people choose this sport? What makes them run such terrible risks? Many climbers have tried to explain it. Andrzej Zawada said he wanted to "conquer" the highest peaks. Roger Mear said that to succeed when "chances are limited—that's what mountaineering is all about." Giusto Gervasutti called mountain climbing "an inner need." He said it showed "the freedom of the [human] spirit." But perhaps Alison Hargreaves explained it best. Hargreaves knew that someday she might die on a mountain. But as she put it, "One day as a tiger is better than a thousand as a sheep."

If you have been timed while reading this selection, enter your reading time below. Then turn to the Words-per-Minute table on page 110 and look up your reading speed (words per minute). Enter your reading speed on the graph on page 113.

READING TIME: Unit 5	
_____ : _____	
Minutes	*Seconds*

How Well Did You Read?

- *Complete the four exercises that follow. The directions for each exercise will tell you how to mark your answers.*

- *When you have finished all four exercises, use the answer key on page 106 to check your work. For each right answer, put a check mark (✓) on the line beside the box. For each wrong answer, write the correct answer on the line.*

- *Follow the directions after each exercise to find your scores.*

A FINDING THE MAIN IDEA

A good main idea statement answers two questions: it tells *who* or *what* is the subject of the story, and it answers the understood question *does what?* or *is what?* Look at the three statements below. One expresses the main idea of the story you just read. Another statement is *too broad*; it is vague and doesn't tell much about the topic of the story. The third statement is *too narrow*; it tells about only one part of the story.

Match the statements with the three answer choices below by writing the letter of each answer in the box in front of the statement it goes with.

M—Main Idea   B—Too Broad   N—Too Narrow

____ ☐ 1. Falling into a crevasse is only one of the many dangers that people face in climbing high mountains.

____ ☐ 2. Climbing very high mountains presents physical problems and dangers more intense than those found in regular mountain climbing.

____ ☐ 3. Climbing mountains takes extraordinary skill, strength, and mental toughness.

____ Score 15 points for a correct *M* answer.
____ Score 5 points for each correct *B* or *N* answer.

____ TOTAL SCORE: Finding the Main Idea

B RECALLING FACTS

How well do you remember the facts in the story you just read? Put an *x* in the box in front of the correct answer to each of the multiple-choice questions below.

1. The signs of altitude sickness include
   ____ ☐ a. dizziness, a bloody nose, and vomiting.
   ____ ☐ b. severe headaches.
   ____ ☐ c. inability to see well and loss of memory.

2. Fischer and Viesturs, swept away by an avalanche, were saved when
   ____ ☐ a. a helicopter rescued them.
   ____ ☐ b. their ropes stopped their fall.
   ____ ☐ c. Viesturs dug his ice ax into the ground and stopped their fall.

3. Crevasses are particularly hard to spot because
   ____ ☐ a. they are so deep.
   ____ ☐ b. they are often covered by fresh snow.
   ____ ☐ c. the sunlight reflects off them confusingly.

4. Peggy Luce was the second American woman to
   ____ ☐ a. climb to the top of K2.
   ____ ☐ b. reach the top of Mount Whitney.
   ____ ☐ c. reach the top of Mount Everest.

5. Snow blindness is caused by
   ____ ☐ a. very heavy snowstorms.
   ____ ☐ b. the glare of sunlight reflecting off the snow.
   ____ ☐ c. strong winds blowing the snow around.

Score 5 points for each correct answer.

____ TOTAL SCORE: Recalling Facts

C MAKING INFERENCES

When you use information from the text and your own experience to draw a conclusion that is not directly stated in the text, you are making an *inference*.

Below are five statements that may or may *not* be inferences based on the facts of the story. Write the letter *C* in the box in front of each statement that is a correct inference. Write the letter *F* in front of each faulty inference.

C—Correct Inference   F—Faulty Inference

____ ☐ 1. Climbers who tackle very high mountains should have strong and healthy lungs.

____ ☐ 2. Most people need plenty of oxygen to think clearly.

____ ☐ 3. After you reach the top of a mountain, you can be sure that the worst of the dangers are over.

____ ☐ 4. Winds at the top of a mountain are often stronger than they are in the valley below it.

____ ☐ 5. The best way to climb a high mountain is to go by yourself so you can travel quickly.

Score 5 points for each correct *C* or *F* answer.

____ TOTAL SCORE: Making Inferences

USING WORDS PRECISELY

Each numbered sentence below contains an underlined word or phrase from the story you just read. Following the sentence are three definitions. One is a *synonym* for the underlined word, one is an *antonym*, and one has a completely *different* meaning than the underlined word.

For each definition, write the letter that stands for the correct answer in the box.

S—Synonym   A—Antonym   D—Different

1. As your brain becomes <u>starved for</u> oxygen, you may find yourself getting dizzy and confused.

____ ☐ a. filled with

____ ☐ b. extremely hungry for

____ ☐ c. aware of

2. This <u>altitude</u> sickness is no joke.

____ ☐ a. depth

____ ☐ b. climbing

____ ☐ c. height

3. That is a <u>classic</u> problem on these mountains.

____ ☐ a. typical

____ ☐ b. dangerous

____ ☐ c. unusual

4. Winds also pose a <u>threat</u>.

____ ☐ a. promise of future safety

____ ☐ b. fear

____ ☐ c. suggestion of coming danger

5. All night, <u>fierce</u> gusts swirled around the mountain.

____ ☐ a. violent

____ ☐ b. mild

____ ☐ c. cold

____ Score 3 points for a correct *S* answer.
____ Score 1 point for each correct *A* or *D* answer.

____ TOTAL SCORE: Using Words Precisely

• *Enter the total score for each exercise in the spaces below. Add the scores to find your Critical Reading Score. Then record your Critical Reading Score on the graph on page 114.*

_____ Finding the Main Idea
_____ Recalling Facts
_____ Making Inferences
_____ Using Words Precisely

_____ CRITICAL READING SCORE: Unit 5

Group Two.

Why is the horse at the right jumping? In any other race, you might think it got confused. But this is the Palio, where anything goes. Perhaps the flash of gunpowder that started the race startled the horse. Perhaps its jockey urged the horse to jump, to knock another jockey off his mount. Or maybe the horse just soaked up too much of the excitement surrounding this wild race—the excitement that has been drawing thousands of fans to Sienna, Italy, for over 700 years.

THE WORLD'S WILDEST HORSE RACE

There is no other race in the world like it. It is older than the Kentucky Derby. It is wilder than a three-ring circus. And it is more colorful than halftime at the Super Bowl.

The race is the Palio. It is held twice each year in Siena, Italy. The Palio is a horse race with a history going back more than seven hundred years. It pits the city's seventeen districts, or *contrade*, against each other. Each *contrada* has its own flag and its own symbol: the Goose, Wolf, Ram, Snail, and so on. And the rivalries are bitter. "The Palio is a serious matter," said one man who lives in Siena. "It's the very life of our contrada."

Neighborhood pride runs deep for the people of Siena. Loyalty to one's contrada affects all parts of life. Take, for instance, a woman who—for whatever reason—is about to give birth outside her contrada. Pots of dirt from her district will be rushed to her. These will then be used to support the four legs of her bed. In this way the new baby will be born on home soil. The baby will be baptized twice—once into the church and once into the

contrada. When a son marries, it will be in the contrada church. And when he dies, his body will be wrapped in the flag of the contrada.

So this is no ordinary race. Some money is bet on the race, but pride is really what's at stake. Everyone wants his or her contrada to win. But winning the Palio isn't easy. First, only ten horses can run in the race. That means that seven contrade are not even in the event. The ten lucky ones who do race are chosen by lot. Second, the contrade don't get to pick their own horses. Those, too, are chosen by lot. So the horse that won the Palio last year may be racing for a different contrada this year.

Once the horses are assigned, the real fun begins. Each contrada treats its horse like a king. As one man said, "The animal is everything in the Palio." The horse is pampered in every way possible. No one takes any chances with the animal's health. In fact, each horse is guarded day and night. Why? Well, although it's illegal to drug a horse, such tricks have been tried in the past. On the day of the race, each horse is taken to the church

of its contrada. There it is blessed and sprinkled with holy water.

The jockeys who ride these horses are professionals. They come from all over Italy. Each contrada hires the best jockey it can find. The jockeys are in the race just for the money. So they will work for whatever contrada makes them the best offer. That contrada is not always the one that hired them in the first place. You see, the Palio is the most corrupt horse race in the world. In the United States it is illegal to fix a horse race. In Siena it's a tradition!

The people of one contrada often try to bribe other jockeys to lose the race on purpose. To prevent that, each contrada hires a guard to watch its rider. But then the guard might be bribed. So each contrada has to hire a second guard to watch over the first one. This scheming goes on right up until the start of the race.

On the day of the race, there is a huge parade. Marchers from each contrada parade through the city streets. Flag bearers lead the way. They are followed by young men dressed in wigs and medieval clothes. Then comes the jockey, dressed as a knight

Sienna's parade on the day of the Palio features flag bearers in medieval dress, knights in armor, and, of course, the racehorses.

in shining armor. He is followed by a boy leading the contrada's racehorse. At last, the parade ends. Each knight casts off his armor and hops onto his horse. The race is about to begin.

The Palio is held in the heart of the city on July 2 and August 16. The horses race around the edge of a brick-paved square called the Piazza del Campo. The course is dangerous. It contains two sharp turns and lies on the pitch of a hillside. The horses must go around the course three times to win. The winner is the first horse to cross the finish line—with or without a jockey! The prize is the Palio, a silk banner bearing the image of the Virgin Mary.

The race itself is a wild affair. The jockeys must ride bareback. They wear steel helmets for protection. The horses line up behind a rope. The starter drops a match onto some loose gunpowder. BOOM! The rope drops and the horses and jockeys leap into action. At this point, anything goes. The jockeys can—and do—whip each other. They may slam each other into walls, many of which are covered with mattresses to avoid serious injuries. Sometimes horses and jockeys are knocked to the ground. A fallen jockey might then stand on the track and try to knock down other jockeys.

Meanwhile, the seventy thousand fans jammed into the piazza go wild. People faint from all the excitement. Dozens of fights break out in the stands. When the race ends, citizens from the winning contrada cheer loudly. They rush to hug the jockey and caress the horse. They then march through the streets of the city, boasting and taunting. The winning contrada will party all through the night. The losers can't wait for the next Palio—and revenge.

If you have been timed while reading this selection, enter your reading time below. Then turn to the Words-per-Minute table on page 111 and look up your reading speed (words per minute). Enter your reading speed on the graph on page 113.

READING TIME: Unit 6
_____ : _____
Minutes   *Seconds*

How Well Did You Read?

- *Complete the four exercises that follow. The directions for each exercise will tell you how to mark your answers.*

- *When you have finished all four exercises, use the answer key on page 107 to check your work. For each right answer, put a check mark (✓) on the line beside the box. For each wrong answer, write the correct answer on the line.*

- *Follow the directions after each exercise to find your scores.*

A FINDING THE MAIN IDEA

A good main idea statement answers two questions: it tells *who* or *what* is the subject of the story, and it answers the understood question *does what?* or *is what?* Look at the three statements below. One expresses the main idea of the story you just read. Another statement is *too broad*; it is vague and doesn't tell much about the topic of the story. The third statement is *too narrow*; it tells about only one part of the story.

Match the statements with the three answer choices below by writing the letter of each answer in the box in front of the statement it goes with.

M—Main Idea   B—Too Broad   N—Too Narrow

_____ ☐ 1. Horse racing has been one of the world's most popular sports for hundreds of years, and the Palio of Siena, Italy, is one of the oldest horse races.

_____ ☐ 2. The Palio of Siena, Italy, a horse race held twice a year, is a good-natured rivalry where the only rule is that almost anything goes.

_____ ☐ 3. On the day of the Palio, a famous horse race of Siena, each horse is taken to its contrada's church to be blessed and sprinkled with holy water.

_____ Score 15 points for a correct *M* answer.
_____ Score 5 points for each correct *B* or *N* answer.

_____ TOTAL SCORE: Finding the Main Idea

B RECALLING FACTS

How well do you remember the facts in the story you just read? Put an *x* in the box in front of the correct answer to each of the multiple-choice questions below.

1. The contrade that compete in the Palio are the
   - ☐ a. most important families of Siena.
   - ☐ b. town's major business interests.
   - ☐ c. ancient districts of the city.

2. Horses are assigned to run for the various contrade
   - ☐ a. by a lottery.
   - ☐ b. by a complicated scheduling system.
   - ☐ c. through bribery.

3. People in Siena expect every jockey to
   - ☐ a. train hard for this event.
   - ☐ b. accept bribes from several contrade.
   - ☐ c. remain loyal to one contrada for life.

4. The race is held
   - ☐ a. on a racecourse just outside of town.
   - ☐ b. on a racecourse within the city walls.
   - ☐ c. in the Piazza del Campo.

5. In order to win, a horse must
   - ☐ a. circle the piazza three times and reach the finish line first, with or without its jockey.
   - ☐ b. carry its rider, wearing full armor, to the finish line.
   - ☐ c. try to bump into other horses during the race.

Score 5 points for each correct answer.

_____ TOTAL SCORE: Recalling Facts

C MAKING INFERENCES

When you use information from the text and your own experience to draw a conclusion that is not directly stated in the text, you are making an *inference*.

Below are five statements that may or may *not* be inferences based on the facts of the story. Write the letter C in the box in front of each statement that is a correct inference. Write the letter F in front of each faulty inference.

C—Correct Inference   F—Faulty Inference

1. Most natives of Siena's contrade frequently move from one district of the city to another.

2. Citizens of a contrada trust their horse to do its best much more than they trust the contrada's jockey to do so.

3. The people of Siena would agree that moving the race to a new, state-of-the-art racecourse would make the Palio even more exciting.

4. Jockeys may make more money when they lose the Palio than when they win.

5. Only tourists interested in the Palio should take rooms next to the Piazza del Campo for the dates of the race.

Score 5 points for each correct C or F answer.

_____ TOTAL SCORE: Making Inferences

USING WORDS PRECISELY

Each numbered sentence below contains an underlined word or phrase from the story you just read. Following the sentence are three definitions. One is a *synonym* for the underlined word, one is an *antonym*, and one has a completely *different* meaning than the underlined word.

For each definition, write the letter that stands for the correct answer in the box.

S—Synonym   A—Antonym   D—Different

1. <u>Loyalty</u> to one's contrada affects all parts of life.
   ____ ☐ a. closeness
   ____ ☐ b. betrayal
   ____ ☐ c. faithfulness

2. Once the horses are <u>assigned</u>, the real fun begins.
   ____ ☐ a. given out
   ____ ☐ b. taken back
   ____ ☐ c. set aside

3. The horse is <u>pampered</u> in every way possible.
   ____ ☐ a. trained
   ____ ☐ b. spoiled
   ____ ☐ c. punished

4. You see, the Palio is the most <u>corrupt</u> horse race in the world.
   ____ ☐ a. dishonest
   ____ ☐ b. pure
   ____ ☐ c. dangerous

5. The course is dangerous. It contains two sharp turns and lies on the <u>pitch</u> of the hillside.
   ____ ☐ a. rise
   ____ ☐ b. slope
   ____ ☐ c. value

____ Score 3 points for a correct *S* answer.
____ Score 1 point for each correct *A* or *D* answer.

____ TOTAL SCORE: Using Words Precisely

• *Enter the total score for each exercise in the spaces below. Add the scores to find your Critical Reading Score. Then record your Critical Reading Score on the graph on page 114.*

_____ Finding the Main Idea
_____ Recalling Facts
_____ Making Inferences
_____ Using Words Precisely

_____ CRITICAL READING SCORE: Unit 6

No, these skiers did not take wrong turns and wind up in the wrong place. They MEANT to ski in these frightening situations! They have taken up the most dangerous form of skiing, called extreme skiing. Before they jump off heights or slide down mountain sides, extreme skiers examine the areas carefully. They make sure that there is a safe path and that they will not be surprised by hidden dangers on the way down.

SKIING THE IMPOSSIBLE

Is Kristen Ulmer out of her mind? You might think so when she describes some of the jumps she's made on skis. For instance, there was the time she flew through the air so out of control that she fainted from fear. Luckily, she didn't kill herself. But she did crash into a tree. Still, Ulmer didn't quit skiing. Instead, she went out looking for even bigger jumps.

Ulmer is one of a small band of extreme skiers who feel they have outgrown normal skiing. Normal ski trails are marked. Signs tell everyone how hard the different trails are. Green circles are easy paths for "snow bunnies." Blue squares are harder, but they can be skied by most good skiers. Black diamonds are steep trails for experts only. Black diamonds offer plenty of excitement for most people. But not for Kristen Ulmer and friends. To them, all marked trails look too tame. They want to ski the impossible!

What qualifies as "impossible"? You can take your pick. Some extreme skiers love to ski off cliffs. A man named Terry Cook does backflips off 60-foot cliffs. Others like to ski in the narrow openings between cliffs. Scott

Schmidt is known for skiing along thin strips of snow that cut through the mountains of Italy. He zips through passageways with huge walls of rock on either side. Sometimes the passageways are no more than 10 feet wide. One slip and he'll smash into the rocks. "It's like skiing through a twisted cave," Schmidt says. "The light is dim and far above you, and the rock walls blur as you rocket past."

Others enjoy the thrill of skiing down a glacier in Antarctica. Some, meanwhile, choose to ski the summits of huge mountains in Asia. You get the point: extreme skiers live to prove that what seems impossible really can be done.

Once a slope has been conquered, extreme skiers often move on to something else. The idea is to find a place that no one has ever skied before. Scott Schmidt does that. As he climbs up cliffs, he is always searching for "something tougher." As Schmidt says, "I [spend] all that energy hauling my skis up there, and I [don't] want to waste it just repeating the old stuff."

Pierre Tardivel, a top extreme skier from France, feels the same way. "I'm

not interested if something *has* been done," he says. "I want to know if it *can* be done. That's the adventure."

Tardivel has skied nearly fifty "firsts." He was the first to ski the south summit of Mount Everest. At 28,766 feet, that's higher than anyone on skis had ever been. Tardivel is an expert at skiing down steep terrain. Most black diamond trails have slopes no steeper than 30 degrees. Tardivel skis slopes of 45 to 60 degrees! Imagine standing up straight on such a steep slope. At 45 degrees you could reach out and touch the snow with your hand. At 60 degrees you could touch it with your elbow!

Tardivel takes his time when he skis a new place. He doesn't simply tuck and race down. That would be suicide. Instead, he picks his way along, making one or two turns at a time. He has to plan every move. That way he can avoid ice and boulders that often litter the run. Even so, he usually slides 50 feet or more before the edges of his skis grab enough to stop.

People can die skiing the "impossible." Tardivel knows that

better than most. And he says he doesn't want to die. There is a saying in extreme sports: "Live and learn; learn or die." So Tardivel always climbs up a new run before he skis down it. When asked why, he answers, "Gouvy and Moroni."

Bruno Gouvy and Alain Moroni were extreme skiers. Both died because they didn't climb up a new run before they skied down it. Gouvy took a helicopter to the summit of a mountain in France. He didn't know there was black ice beneath the snow. He slipped and fell to his death. Moroni rode a ski lift to a summit and walked over to a new place he wanted to try. He, too, fell to his death. "Both were killed because they started from the top," says Tardivel.

Why do extreme skiers risk their lives in the first place? To most of us, it seems they must have a death wish. But they deny that. They say it isn't a matter of courting death. It's a matter of facing your fears and overcoming them. That's why Scott Schmidt became interested in the sport. As a child, Schmidt liked to be pulled along behind his father's snowmobile. One day his father tried to take him over a "monster two-foot jump." Recalls Scott, "I chickened out and let go of the rope right on the lip. That's when I started confronting my fears."

The best way to do that, he found, was by extreme skiing.

Conquering your fear is not the same as losing your fear. In fact, extreme skiers say the fear is always there. "You've got to have some fear of what you're doing or else you don't belong out there," declares extreme skier Dean Cummings.

"We all know extreme skiing is dangerous," echoes Kristen Ulmer. But she insists it's worth the risks. For her, it's about "the need to be the best you can be and to express that through what you do." Also, Ulmer says, extreme skiing helps you believe in yourself. You become your own superhero. You learn to have complete faith in your abilities. That faith, she says, "is absolutely essential if you want to be an extreme skier."

Extreme skiers now compete against each other. Every year they face off in the World Extreme Skiing Championship. This event is not open to everyone. You have to be well prepared. You have to prove that you have skied at least four extreme descents. Skiers must be expert mountain climbers. And they must be trained in avoiding and surviving avalanches.

In the championship, the skiers are taken to the top of some wild peak. As they ski down, judges grade them on style and difficulty. If you win—great. But just staying alive is also a triumph. In 1993 a skier died when the snow ledge he was on gave way. For safety, skiers must wear avalanche beacons. That makes it possible for rescuers to locate them and try to save them.

Dean Cummings once barely escaped death. He was caught in an avalanche and almost tumbled over a 100-foot cliff. What did he think about his brush with death? It was a contest between sheer fright and wild fun. And fun won. Cummings calls his experience "the most incredible buzz you could ever have." It's thoughts like this that make Ulmer, Tardivel, and Cummings "extreme." The rest of us can find plenty of "buzz" on regular ski trails.

If you have been timed while reading this selection, enter your reading time below. Then turn to the Words-per-Minute table on page 111 and look up your reading speed (words per minute). Enter your reading speed on the graph on page 113.

READING TIME: Unit 7	
_____ : _____	
Minutes	*Seconds*

How Well Did You Read?

- *Complete the four exercises that follow. The directions for each exercise will tell you how to mark your answers.*

- *When you have finished all four exercises, use the answer key on page 107 to check your work. For each right answer, put a check mark (✓) on the line beside the box. For each wrong answer, write the correct answer on the line.*

- *Follow the directions after each exercise to find your scores.*

 **FINDING THE MAIN IDEA**

A good main idea statement answers two questions: it tells *who* or *what* is the subject of the story, and it answers the understood question *does what?* or *is what?* Look at the three statements below. One expresses the main idea of the story you just read. Another statement is *too broad*; it is vague and doesn't tell much about the topic of the story. The third statement is *too narrow*; it tells about only one part of the story.

Match the statements with the three answer choices below by writing the letter of each answer in the box in front of the statement it goes with.

M—Main Idea   B—Too Broad   N—Too Narrow

____ ☐ 1. Extreme skiing, that is, skiing in areas that are usually considered impossible to ski, is a sport that requires strength and daring.

____ ☐ 2. People who like excitement and the chance to test their own personal limits would enjoy extreme skiing.

____ ☐ 3. Extreme skier Pierre Tardivel was the first to ski the south summit of Mount Everest.

____ Score 15 points for a correct *M* answer.
____ Score 5 points for each correct *B* or *N* answer.

____ TOTAL SCORE: Finding the Main Idea

B RECALLING FACTS

How well do you remember the facts in the story you just read? Put an *x* in the box in front of the correct answer to each of the multiple-choice questions below.

1. A black diamond on a trail marker means that the trail is
   - ___ ☐ a. easy enough for beginners.
   - ___ ☐ b. possible for most good skiers.
   - ___ ☐ c. full of steep places for expert skiers only.

2. Extreme skier Pierre Tardivel always climbs a new run before he skis down it, because he
   - ___ ☐ a. enjoys mountain climbing as much as skiing.
   - ___ ☐ b. wants to learn about its hazards.
   - ___ ☐ c. is afraid of ski lifts.

3. A slope of 45 degrees would be
   - ___ ☐ a. easy to ski.
   - ___ ☐ b. good for an expert skier.
   - ___ ☐ c. fit only for an extreme skier to try.

4. Judges grade extreme skiers on their
   - ___ ☐ a. style and the difficulty of the descent.
   - ___ ☐ b. speed in coming down the mountain.
   - ___ ☐ c. attention to safety rules.

5. Skiers wear avalanche beacons because beacons
   - ___ ☐ a. make it easier for the judges to see them.
   - ___ ☐ b. will help rescuers locate them.
   - ___ ☐ c. can keep the skiers warm.

Score 5 points for each correct answer.

___ TOTAL SCORE: Recalling Facts

C MAKING INFERENCES

When you use information from the text and your own experience to draw a conclusion that is not directly stated in the text, you are making an *inference*.

Below are five statements that may or may *not* be inferences based on the facts of the story. Write the letter *C* in the box in front of each statement that is a correct inference. Write the letter *F* in front of each faulty inference.

C—Correct Inference   **F—Faulty Inference**

1. ___ ☐ Most of the time, extreme skiers would welcome a group of inexperienced skiers to join them on their mountain runs.

2. ___ ☐ Skier Pierre Tardivel has climbed the south summit of Mount Everest.

3. ___ ☐ If extreme skiers didn't ski, they probably would find another way to test their strength and courage.

4. ___ ☐ A person with little self-confidence would be most likely to take up extreme skiing.

5. ___ ☐ The organizers of the World Extreme Skiing Championship are concerned about the safety of the skiers.

Score 5 points for each correct *C* or *F* answer.

___ TOTAL SCORE: Making Inferences

D USING WORDS PRECISELY

Each numbered sentence below contains an underlined word or phrase from the story you just read. Following the sentence are three definitions. One is a *synonym* for the underlined word, one is an *antonym*, and one has a completely *different* meaning than the underlined word.

For each definition, write the letter that stands for the correct answer in the box.

S—Synonym   A—Antonym   D—Different

1. That way he can avoid ice and boulders that often <u>litter</u> the run.

____ ☐ a. make clean and orderly

____ ☐ b. build

____ ☐ c. clutter up

2. Moroni rode a ski lift to a <u>summit</u> and walked over to a new place he wanted to try.

____ ☐ a. hotel

____ ☐ b. highest point

____ ☐ c. lowest point

3. They say it isn't a matter of <u>courting</u> death.

____ ☐ a. working to attract

____ ☐ b. trying to avoid

____ ☐ c. understanding

4. He doesn't simply <u>tuck</u> and race down.

____ ☐ a. crouch

____ ☐ b. look carefully

____ ☐ c. stretch out

5. But just staying alive is also a <u>triumph</u>.

____ ☐ a. surprise

____ ☐ b. defeat

____ ☐ c. victory

____ Score 3 points for a correct *S* answer.

____ Score 1 point for each correct *A* or *D* answer.

____ TOTAL SCORE: Using Words Precisely

• *Enter the total score for each exercise in the spaces below. Add the scores to find your Critical Reading Score. Then record your Critical Reading Score on the graph on page 114.*

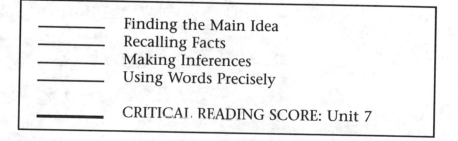

_____ Finding the Main Idea

_____ Recalling Facts

_____ Making Inferences

_____ Using Words Precisely

_____ CRITICAL READING SCORE: Unit 7

Many people respect the courage of bullfighters. Some people even choose to imitate the fighters' courage by joining in the annual Running of the Bulls in Pamplona, Spain. But a few, like this man, discover painfully that the risks are as real as the romance.

RUNNING WITH THE BULLS

What's the greatest adventure you could ever have? As writer James Michener put it, "You can climb Mount Everest, fly to the moon, or run with the bulls at Pamplona." The first two things require special training and a lot of money. But running with the bulls is something ordinary people can do . . . *if they dare.*

The Running of the Bulls takes place in Pamplona, Spain, each July. For eight days in a row, bulls are released into the streets of the city. These are not baby bulls. They are full-grown, 1,300-pound animals. They have sharp hooves and deadly horns. And they can run like the wind. As the bulls tear through the streets, they are joined by over a thousand people. These people want the thrill of running alongside the bulls. They hope to get close to them. But every year some people get a little too close. They end up being trampled, gored, even killed by the frenzied bulls.

The Running of the Bulls has been going on for about three hundred years. It began for a very practical reason. Each July, bullfights are held in Pamplona's bullring. The fights are part of a festival called Fiesta de San Fermín. The bullring is half a mile from the corral where the bulls are kept. Somehow, then, the bulls have to be moved from the corral to the bullring. The people of Pamplona came up with a simple solution. They began herding the animals right through the streets.

It wasn't long before a few brave souls chose to run along with the bulls. These people wanted to test their speed. They also wanted to prove their fearlessness. And so, the Running of the Bulls was born.

Now the Running of the Bulls is the most famous part of the San Fermín festival. People come from all over the world to take part in it. The runners wear red bandannas. The bravest ones also carry rolled-up newspapers. These newspapers are called "Pamplona Badges of Honor." They show which runners intend to get close to the bulls. Runners who carry a newspaper feel their honor is lost if they do not at least touch a bull with their "badge."

The event begins at exactly 8 A.M. A rocket is fired and the gates of the corral open. Six angry bulls charge out. Along with them come several steers used to keep the bulls going in the right direction.

Sometimes everything goes smoothly. The bulls stick together and run straight ahead. They ignore the swarms of people racing all around them. On those days, the bulls reach the bullring within two or three minutes. There they are safely penned up until that night's bullfight.

But things do not always go smoothly. Sometimes one of the bulls breaks away from the pack. It becomes confused. It swings around, tossing its giant horns. Furious, it may attack just about anything it sees.

The runners who happen to be near such a bull are in big trouble. They are trapped in a narrow street with no escape. Some try to hide in doorways. Others stand motionless, hoping the bull will not notice them. Many keep running. But as one runner said, "If you think you can outrun [the bulls], you're making a big mistake."

James Michener was running with the bulls in 1969 when one broke away from the pack. For some reason, this bull suddenly turned right. In a blind rage, it charged at a group of runners. Michener described the results. "A dreadful thing has occurred. The bull's right horn has ripped into the unprotected stomach of a well-known runner named Gregorio Zamora Irazabal. He was running about eight feet from me and I saw the horn cut him open like a boy unzipping a shirt. His belly was laid bare and his guts spilled into the street."

Next, Michener wrote, the bull turned to a second man. "With sickening force the bull [slammed] his right horn into the man's stomach. Then, with powerful thrust of head, he [ripped] the horn upward through the chest." At last, "the deadly bull, his horns tipped with the blood of two men, [rejoined] his herd."

This was not the first time someone died in the Running of the Bulls. Since 1924, more than a dozen people have lost their lives in the event. Hundreds more have been injured. The Spanish Red Cross estimates that thirty to forty people are hurt each day the bulls run. Some suffer only minor injuries. They may fall in the street and bruise a shoulder. Or they may be knocked against a wall and scrape a knee. Others, however, are more seriously hurt. They may be kicked or stepped on by a bull. And every year, seven or eight people are gored by the bulls' horns.

In 1995, for the first time, an American died during the Running of the Bulls. His name was Matthew Tassio. He was twenty-two years old. Tassio was vacationing in Spain when he decided to run with the bulls. So, early on the morning of July 13, he arrived in Pamplona. When the rocket went off, he began running with the crowd. But he tripped on the cobblestone street. He fell right into the path of an oncoming bull. Tassio tried to get up. But as he did so, the bull tore into him. Its horn pierced his stomach and cut an artery close to his heart. In just a few minutes, Tassio bled to death.

Despite tragedies like this, people continue to run with the bulls. Most say they do it for the sheer excitement of being near the huge beasts. "I do it because I love to be with those animals," said one American. "It's something to feel them thunder past." And so, if you're ever looking for adventure, you might head to Pamplona, Spain, next July. Remember to pack a red bandanna. And be sure your life insurance policy is up to date!

If you have been timed while reading this selection, enter your reading time below. Then turn to the Words-per-Minute table on page 111 and look up your reading speed (words per minute). Enter your reading speed on the graph on page 113.

READING TIME: Unit 8	
_____ : _____	
Minutes	*Seconds*

How Well Did You Read?

- *Complete the four exercises that follow. The directions for each exercise will tell you how to mark your answers.*

- *When you have finished all four exercises, use the answer key on page 107 to check your work. For each right answer, put a check mark (✓) on the line beside the box. For each wrong answer, write the correct answer on the line.*

- *Follow the directions after each exercise to find your scores.*

 FINDING THE MAIN IDEA

A good main idea statement answers two questions: it tells *who* or *what* is the subject of the story, and it answers the understood question *does what?* or *is what?* Look at the three statements below. One expresses the main idea of the story you just read. Another statement is *too broad*; it is vague and doesn't tell much about the topic of the story. The third statement is *too narrow*; it tells about only one part of the story.

Match the statements with the three answer choices below by writing the letter of each answer in the box in front of the statement it goes with.

M—Main Idea   B—Too Broad   N—Too Narrow

____ ☐ 1. Running alongside the bulls as they are moved from the corral to the bullring in Pamplona, Spain, has become an exciting and dangerous sport.

____ ☐ 2. The yearly festival in Pamplona, Spain, always includes the Running of the Bulls.

____ ☐ 3. The bravest runners carry newspapers with which they touch the bulls as they run through the streets.

____ Score 15 points for a correct *M* answer.
____ Score 5 points for each correct *B* or *N* answer.

____ TOTAL SCORE: Finding the Main Idea

B RECALLING FACTS

How well do you remember the facts in the story you just read? Put an *x* in the box in front of the correct answer to each of the multiple-choice questions below.

1. The Running of the Bulls takes place during the
   - ☐ a. winter.
   - ☐ b. summer.
   - ☐ c. spring.

2. Several steers are released along with the bulls to
   - ☐ a. keep the bulls going in the right direction.
   - ☐ b. slow the bulls down.
   - ☐ c. prepare people for the bulls.

3. Bulls often attack runners because the bulls
   - ☐ a. are confused and frightened.
   - ☐ b. hate all people.
   - ☐ c. want to eat the runners.

4. One year, writer James Michener saw the bulls
   - ☐ a. break windows.
   - ☐ b. kill two men.
   - ☐ c. refuse to run through the city streets.

5. To signal the release of the bulls from the corral, a
   - ☐ a. cannon is fired.
   - ☐ b. loud horn is blown.
   - ☐ c. rocket is fired.

Score 5 points for each correct answer.

____ TOTAL SCORE: Recalling Facts

C MAKING INFERENCES

When you use information from the text and your own experience to draw a conclusion that is not directly stated in the text, you are making an *inference*.

Below are five statements that may or may *not* be inferences based on the facts of the story. Write the letter *C* in the box in front of each statement that is a correct inference. Write the letter *F* in front of each faulty inference.

C—Correct Inference   F—Faulty Inference

1. The bulls used in bullfights are usually angry bulls.

2. The people of Pamplona, Spain, are happy with their tradition of the Running of the Bulls.

3. Only citizens of Spain are allowed to run with the bulls.

4. The Spanish Red Cross probably does not recommend the sport of running with the bulls.

5. If someone died while trying to run with the bulls next year, city officials would probably stop the tradition.

Score 5 points for each correct *C* or *F* answer.

____ TOTAL SCORE: Making Inferences

USING WORDS PRECISELY

Each numbered sentence below contains an underlined word or phrase from the story you just read. Following the sentence are three definitions. One is a *synonym* for the underlined word, one is an *antonym*, and one has a completely *different* meaning than the underlined word.

For each definition, write the letter that stands for the correct answer in the box.

S—Synonym   A—Antonym   D—Different

1. They end up being trampled, gored, even killed by the <u>frenzied</u> bulls.

_____ ☐ a. wildly excited

_____ ☐ b. calm

_____ ☐ c. strong

2. They <u>ignore</u> the swarms of people racing all around them.

_____ ☐ a. are angry with

_____ ☐ b. pay no attention to

_____ ☐ c. pay close attention to

3. Others stand <u>motionless</u>, hoping the bull will not notice them.

_____ ☐ a. moving constantly

_____ ☐ b. without feelings

_____ ☐ c. without moving

4. A <u>dreadful</u> thing has occurred.

_____ ☐ a. unexpected

_____ ☐ b. wonderful

_____ ☐ c. terrible

5. In a blind rage, it <u>charged</u> a group of runners.

_____ ☐ a. protected against harm

_____ ☐ b. rushed, attacked

_____ ☐ c. saw

_____ Score 3 points for a correct *S* answer.
_____ Score 1 point for each correct *A* or *D* answer.

_____ TOTAL SCORE: Using Words Precisely

• *Enter the total score for each exercise in the spaces below. Add the scores to find your Critical Reading Score. Then record your Critical Reading Score on the graph on page 114.*

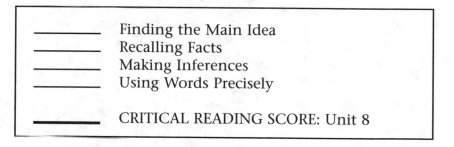

_____ Finding the Main Idea
_____ Recalling Facts
_____ Making Inferences
_____ Using Words Precisely

_____ CRITICAL READING SCORE: Unit 8

A famous stunt flyer of his day, who also starred in silent movies, was Ormer Leslie Locklear. In this photo from June of 1920, Locklear demonstrates his extraordinary wing-walking skills. Daredevils like Locklear appeared in airshows all around the country in the decade following World War I.

STUNT FLYING

Charles Hamilton was no fool. "We shall all be killed if we stay in the business," he said. Hamilton was lucky. He ended up dying a natural death. But many of his friends died in balls of flames. What "business" was Hamilton in? He was a stunt flier. He and other daredevil pilots enthralled fans with their high-risk moves in the sky.

It all began around 1910. Aviation was new. Many people were thrilled just to see a plane. And when that plane started doing tricks—well, it was better than a trip to the circus. In fact, that was what stunt pilots called their acts: flying circuses.

One of the first great stunt pilots was Lincoln Beachey. He could do amazing things in the flimsy planes of the day. He could, for instance, pick a handkerchief off the airfield with his wing tip. In 1911 Beachey stunned people when he flew *under* the bridge at Niagara Falls. But his boldest stunt was to fly straight up until he ran out of gas. Then, somehow, he glided his "dead" plane safely back to earth.

In 1912 Beachey got a call from Glenn Curtiss. Curtiss made airplanes. He wanted to sell his planes to the U.S. Army. But the Army was not convinced that Curtiss planes could do a tight figure eight. Curtiss wanted to show the Army what his product could really do. So he asked Beachey to fly a demonstration. Beachey flew a tighter figure eight than anyone had ever seen. The next day, Army officials asked Beachey for a favor. They asked him never to fly on an Army airfield again! The reason? They worried that their own pilots would try to copy Beachey's stunt and get killed.

Instead, it was Beachey who got killed. It happened in 1915. He was doing an air show in California. During a difficult trick, the wings on his plane broke. Over fifty thousand fans watched in horror as Beachey's plane spun out of control and crashed.

Still, people kept coming back for more. Air shows really took off after World War I ended in 1918. The Army had trained lots of pilots. Suddenly, these men had nothing to do. Many bought their own planes and became stunt fliers. Planes were cheap in those days—about $600 apiece. And with the war over, there were plenty of planes for sale.

The most popular model was a double-winged plane called a Jenny. It was designed to carry two people. Pilots said this plane could land on a dime. They flew their Jennies from town to town, putting on air shows. They used open farm fields for landing and taking off. At night, they put their airplanes into nearby barns for shelter. These men, plus a few equally bold women pilots, became known as "barnstormers."

People flocked to see the air shows. Many of the stunts were truly death defying. Pilots flew upside down. They did loops close to the ground. Sometimes a pilot took along a partner who jumped out of the plane in the middle of the show. To fans who didn't know what a parachute was, this move came as a real shock!

As the years went by, air shows grew more and more outrageous. Pilots began working with "wing-walkers." These people did all sorts of crazy things on the wings of planes. Gladys Roy wowed people by dancing the Charleston on the upper wing. Mabel Cody often "fell" off a wing. She would save herself by grabbing a cord hanging from the airplane. Then, she would place the cord between her teeth and begin to spin around. People always gasped when they saw this Iron Jaw Spin.

Duke Krantz amazed crowds by hanging from a wing by his toes. One day Krantz really stunned his fans. He climbed to the top wing. Then the pilot went into a steep dive and ended in a full loop. All this time, Krantz remained standing on the wing. A hidden cable held him in place. But for a few moments, the awestruck crowd felt sure he would plunge to his death.

The fact that some pilots *did* fall to their deaths added to the thrill. Laura Bromwell fell out of her cockpit during a loop. She was more than one thousand feet in the air at the time. She did not survive the fall.

Sometimes two pilots would team up. With two planes in the air, wing walkers could really go wild. Ethel Dare, known as the Flying Witch, had a daring trick. She would climb down a rope ladder from one plane, then jump to the wing of a second plane. That act was later banned, however, when a man was killed trying to perform it.

By 1930, air shows were dying out. New laws against low-level flying forced many shows to close. Besides, flying was now seen as serious business. Pilots took on new challenges. Charles Lindbergh started out as a barnstormer. But in 1924 he became an army pilot. Three years later, he made the first flight across the Atlantic Ocean. Clyde "Upside-Down" Pangborn spent years in a flying circus. Then he turned to long-distance flight. In 1931 he made the first nonstop trip across the Pacific.

Still, the attraction of stunt flying never completely died. In recent years, air shows have been on the rise again. Now most shows feature jets, not Jennies. But the element of danger remains. In 1988, German pilots held a big air show. Pilots in nine jets traced a big heart across the sky. A tenth pilot tried to draw a line of smoke straight through the figure. It was supposed to be an arrow piercing the heart. But this tenth jet didn't move fast enough. It hit one of the other planes, causing them both to crash into the crowd. Forty-nine people died.

Lee Oman had a close call in a 1991 air show. Oman liked to perform a trick on an old-fashioned, double-winged plane. He hung from a bar below the plane. He moved his legs as though walking in midair. One day, though, his hands slipped off the bar. He fell ten feet before the harness he was wearing caught him. He dangled helplessly from the harness, having no way to get back up to the bar. The pilot had to drop him onto a speeding truck in order to save his life.

In 1991 Joann Osterud found a way to combine stunt flying and long-distance flying. She set a new record for the longest flight made upside-down. She flew her biplane that way for four hours and thirty-eight minutes. She covered 658 miles. Clearly, in Osterud, Oman, and others like them, the tradition of stunt flying is alive and well.

If you have been timed while reading this selection, enter your reading time below. Then turn to the Words-per-Minute table on page 111 and look up your reading speed (words per minute). Enter your reading speed on the graph on page 113.

READING TIME: Unit 9	
_____ : _____	
Minutes	*Seconds*

How Well Did You Read?

- *Complete the four exercises that follow. The directions for each exercise will tell you how to mark your answers.*

- *When you have finished all four exercises, use the answer key on page 107 to check your work. For each right answer, put a check mark (✓) on the line beside the box. For each wrong answer, write the correct answer on the line.*

- *Follow the directions after each exercise to find your scores.*

A FINDING THE MAIN IDEA

A good main idea statement answers two questions: it tells *who* or *what* is the subject of the story, and it answers the understood question *does what?* or *is what?* Look at the three statements below. One expresses the main idea of the story you just read. Another statement is *too broad*; it is vague and doesn't tell much about the topic of the story. The third statement is *too narrow*; it tells about only one part of the story.

Match the statements with the three answer choices below by writing the letter of each answer in the box in front of the statement it goes with.

M—Main Idea   **B—Too Broad**   **N—Too Narrow**

____ ☐ 1. Since the beginnings of aviation around 1910, stunt fliers have created thrills with their daring piloting, wing-walking, and other moves on planes.

____ ☐ 2. The invention of the airplane at the beginning of the twentieth century opened the skies to adventurous men and women.

____ ☐ 3. Charles Lindbergh, who started his career as a barnstormer, gained fame in 1927 when he made the first flight across the Atlantic Ocean.

____ Score 15 points for a correct *M* answer.
____ Score 5 points for each correct *B* or *N* answer.

____ TOTAL SCORE: Finding the Main Idea

B RECALLING FACTS

How well do you remember the facts in the story you just read? Put an *x* in the box in front of the correct answer to each of the multiple-choice questions below.

1. Lincoln Beachey proved to the U.S. Army that
   - ☐ a. a person could walk on a plane wing.
   - ☐ b. a Curtiss plane could fly a tight figure eight.
   - ☐ c. planes could be used reliably in warfare.

2. After World War I, a small plane cost about
   - ☐ a. $60.
   - ☐ b. $600.
   - ☐ c. $6,000.

3. Mabel Cody pretended to fall off a wing, saved herself by grabbing a cord, and then
   - ☐ a. climbed the cord back up to the wing.
   - ☐ b. dropped to earth with a parachute.
   - ☐ c. put the cord between her teeth and spun.

4. Clyde Pangborn was the first person to fly
   - ☐ a. nonstop from Maine to California.
   - ☐ b. solo across the Atlantic.
   - ☐ c. nonstop across the Pacific.

5. In 1991 Joann Osterud set a new record for the
   - ☐ a. longest flight made upside-down.
   - ☐ b. longest time spent wing-walking.
   - ☐ c. longest flight in a World War I plane.

Score 5 points for each correct answer.

_____ TOTAL SCORE: Recalling Facts

C MAKING INFERENCES

When you use information from the text and your own experience to draw a conclusion that is not directly stated in the text, you are making an *inference*.

Below are five statements that may or may *not* be inferences based on the facts of the story. Write the letter *C* in the box in front of each statement that is a correct inference. Write the letter *F* in front of each faulty inference.

C—Correct Inference   F—Faulty Inference

1. In the early days of flying, there were few laws limiting what could be done with planes.

2. The planes called Jennies required a long and very level runway for taking off and landing.

3. Many early planes did not have seatbelts.

4. Lincoln Beachey would have been happy to become a test pilot.

5. As people become more familiar with planes, they will lose all interest in the stunt flying of today and yesterday.

Score 5 points for each correct *C* or *F* answer.

_____ TOTAL SCORE: Making Inferences

D USING WORDS PRECISELY

Each numbered sentence below contains an underlined word or phrase from the story you just read. Following the sentence are three definitions. One is a *synonym* for the underlined word, one is an *antonym*, and one has a completely *different* meaning than the underlined word.

For each definition, write the letter that stands for the correct answer in the box.

S—Synonym   A—Antonym   D—Different

1. He and other daredevil pilots <u>enthralled</u> fans with their high-risk moves in the sky.

___ ☐ a. repelled, drove away

___ ☐ b. fascinated

___ ☐ c. changed the opinions of

2. He could do amazing things in the <u>flimsy</u> planes of the day.

___ ☐ a. fragile, easily broken

___ ☐ b. small, hard to see

___ ☐ c. strong, well-built

3. Many of the stunts were truly death <u>defying</u>.

___ ☐ a. organizing

___ ☐ b. challenging

___ ☐ c. obeying

4. Gladys Roy <u>wowed</u> people by dancing the Charleston on the upper wing.

___ ☐ a. paid

___ ☐ b. bored

___ ☐ c. dazzled

5. A hidden cable held him in place. But for a few moments, the <u>awestruck</u> crowd felt sure he would plunge to his death.

___ ☐ a. scornful

___ ☐ b. noisy

___ ☐ c. amazed

___ Score 3 points for a correct *S* answer.
___ Score 1 point for each correct *A* or *D* answer.

___ TOTAL SCORE: Using Words Precisely

• *Enter the total score for each exercise in the spaces below. Add the scores to find your Critical Reading Score. Then record your Critical Reading Score on the graph on page 114.*

_____ Finding the Main Idea
_____ Recalling Facts
_____ Making Inferences
_____ Using Words Precisely

_____ CRITICAL READING SCORE: Unit 9

Once the only dependable way to travel over Alaska's snow-covered land was by dogsled. Even today, many settlements cannot be reached by roads; you must take a plane to get from place to place. Before planes, when something absolutely had to get somewhere, it went by dogsled. For example, in 1925, a diphtheria epidemic threatened the northern town of Nome. Medicine had to be carried from Nenana to Nome to save the town. A team led by a valiant dog named Balto triumphed over a blizzard and brought the medicine in time. Today, adventurous racers and their dog teams compete in the Iditarod, a race over the same trail used by Balto and other travelers of a century ago.

THE LAST GREAT RACE ON EARTH

Iditarod racers can be tall or short, young or old, men or women. There's only one thing they cannot be: cowards. If they are, they will never survive this grueling 1,160-mile race.

In the Iditarod, each racer travels alone on a sled pulled by dogs. The idea is to get from one end of Alaska to the other as fast as possible. That means all the racers—or *mushers*, as they are called—push themselves and their dogs to the limit. Sometimes dogs die along the way. Mushers know that they, too, might die. Still, every year people return to run this "Last Great Race on Earth."

The race begins in the city of Anchorage. Mushers harness their best fifteen or twenty sled dogs. They jump onto sleds packed with food and other supplies. Then they head out. The race course follows an old mail route that used to pass through Alaska's mining towns. But since the towns are mostly deserted now, the race is one long trek through the wilderness. Mushers stop at eighteen checkpoints along the way. Otherwise, they have no contact with the outside world until they reach the finish line in Nome.

With luck, the first hours of the race go smoothly. The dogs find their rhythm. The teams catch every twist and turn in the trail. The mushers can settle back and enjoy the snowy silence of the Alaskan frontier.

Sooner or later, though, trouble is bound to arise. The dogs may stumble on rough ground, cutting their paws on razor-sharp slivers of ice. Or the dogs might make a wrong turn. Then a musher may wander miles off the trail. Frozen lakes and rivers can also spell disaster. If the ice is not thick enough, the entire team can fall through, pulling the musher into the icy water. If that happens, there is little chance of getting out alive.

Then there are the storms. Four-time Iditarod winner Susan Butcher knows all about storms. She once hit a blizzard that left thirty-foot high snowdrifts. In 1985, winner Libby Riddles tried to push her way through a terrible storm. Conditions were so bad that for eleven hours she could not move at all. The first time Gary Paulsen tried the Iditarod, he got stuck in "a killing storm."

Paulsen was way out on the trail when the storm hit. He was miles from the nearest checkpoint. "The wind must have been blowing seventy or eighty miles per hour," he later wrote. "I knew it was impossible to do anything but hunker down and try to survive." Paulsen stopped his sled and climbed into his sleeping bag. His dogs lay down in the snow, curling up into tight little balls. Hours later, after the snow finally stopped, Paulsen and the dogs dug themselves out. Then they resumed the race.

Even if mushers avoid blizzards, there is no way to avoid the bitter cold. Temperatures on the trail can drop to fifty or sixty degrees below zero. One musher reported air so cold it froze the batteries in his flashlight. His wooden matches would not light. In weather like that, frostbite sets in quickly. Mushers may arrive at the finish line with frostbitten cheeks, toes, or fingers.

Certain parts of the trail hold special dangers. Farewell Burn is a ninety-two mile stretch of burned-out forest. The winds that whip through there blow all the snow away. So the dogs must pick their way around rocks, blackened stumps, and water holes. One year, Susan Butcher's sled crashed into a tree as she raced through the Burn. Butcher and four of her dogs were hurt in the accident.

For some, the toughest part of the trail is Rainy Pass. Here mushers must steer their sleds along a narrow ledge. One wrong move can send them tumbling to their deaths in a rock-filled gorge. For others, Happy River is the worst. To reach it, mushers have to navigate a five-hundred-foot drop into a canyon. Then, after crossing the river, they have to climb out the other side.

All of these dangers would be hard enough to face in broad daylight on a good night's sleep. But Iditarod mushers travel at night as well as during the day. And they don't get a good night's sleep. In fact, they don't get much sleep at all. They make many short stops to feed their dogs, but that's not a time for sleeping. At checkpoints, they may take a longer break, but even then, there is a lot to do. Mushers need to check their dogs' paws for cuts. They have to rub their dogs' sore muscles. They may also need to repair their sleds or fix a broken harness. Sometimes mushers grab a few hours'

sleep at a checkpoint. But often they stay just a few minutes, then head out again.

By the middle of the race, then, lack of sleep becomes a real issue. Many mushers begin to doze on the sled. They have to trust their dogs to keep running in the right direction. Some exhausted mushers begin to hallucinate. They see things that are not there. Some see imaginary trees or lakes. Gary Paulsen saw everything from his wife to a man in a suit to the coast of California!

Storms, lack of sleep, and frigid temperatures are always part of the race. But once in a while, mushers run into something more. They come across a crazed moose. Gary Paulsen was run over by such a moose. Luckily, Paulsen was not badly hurt. But that same moose killed a dog in another musher's team.

Susan Butcher's team was also attacked by a moose one year. Butcher tried to scare the moose off with an axe. But again and again, the animal tried to trample her dogs. After twenty minutes, musher Dave Halverson happened by. Halverson, who kept a gun in his sled, quickly shot the moose. By then, two of Butcher's dogs

were dead and most of the others were injured. So Butcher was forced to drop out of the race.

Dropping out of the Iditarod is not cause for shame. When things go wrong, even the best mushers have to call it quits. Still, the thrill of crossing that finish line keeps many of them going. In 1995 Doug Swingley set a new speed record for the race. He completed the course in just nine days, two hours, and forty-two minutes. To do that, he averaged well over a hundred miles a day. But even for mushers who take twice as long to finish, the Iditarod is still the thrill of a lifetime.

If you have been timed while reading this selection, enter your reading time below. Then turn to the Words-per-Minute table on page 111 and look up your reading speed (words per minute). Enter your reading speed on the graph on page 113.

READING TIME: Unit 10	
_____ : _____	
Minutes	*Seconds*

How Well Did You Read?

- *Complete the four exercises that follow. The directions for each exercise will tell you how to mark your answers.*

- *When you have finished all four exercises, use the answer key on page 107 to check your work. For each right answer, put a check mark (✓) on the line beside the box. For each wrong answer, write the correct answer on the line.*

- *Follow the directions after each exercise to find your scores.*

A | FINDING THE MAIN IDEA

A good main idea statement answers two questions: it tells *who* or *what* is the subject of the story, and it answers the understood question *does what?* or *is what?* Look at the three statements below. One expresses the main idea of the story you just read. Another statement is *too broad*; it is vague and doesn't tell much about the topic of the story. The third statement is *too narrow*; it tells about only one part of the story.

Match the statements with the three answer choices below by writing the letter of each answer in the box in front of the statement it goes with.

M—Main Idea   B—Too Broad   N—Too Narrow

____ ☐ 1. In the Iditarod, exhausted racers often fall asleep or see imaginary things along the trail, and their dogs must move forward without direction.

____ ☐ 2. Weariness, bad weather, and hazards along the trail make the Iditarod sled race across Alaska a great but thrilling challenge to each racer.

____ ☐ 3. There are few races anywhere in the world more thrilling than the annual Iditarod dogsled race in Alaska.

____ Score 15 points for a correct *M* answer.
____ Score 5 points for each correct *B* or *N* answer.

____ TOTAL SCORE: Finding the Main Idea

B RECALLING FACTS

How well do you remember the facts in the story you just read? Put an *x* in the box in front of the correct answer to each of the multiple-choice questions below.

1. The Iditarod sled race begins in the city of
   ____ ☐ a. Nome.
   ____ ☐ b. Anchorage.
   ____ ☐ c. Fairbanks.

2. During the race, mushers must stop at
   ____ ☐ a. dusk.
   ____ ☐ b. fifteen checkpoints.
   ____ ☐ c. eighteen checkpoints.

3. Each team consists of
   ____ ☐ a. one racer and a dozen or more dogs.
   ____ ☐ b. one main racer, his or her alternate, and a dozen or more dogs.
   ____ ☐ c. one racer, a dozen or more dogs, and a support crew that brings in fresh dogs.

4. When Gary Paulsen was caught in a blizzard, he
   ____ ☐ a. waited it out in a deserted mining town.
   ____ ☐ b. lay down in the snow until the storm ended.
   ____ ☐ c. had to quit the race.

5. Once, two of Susan Butcher's dogs were killed
   ____ ☐ a. by a powerful and angry moose.
   ____ ☐ b. when they fell through thin ice on a lake.
   ____ ☐ c. when they lost their footing in a canyon.

Score 5 points for each correct answer.

____ TOTAL SCORE: Recalling Facts

C MAKING INFERENCES

When you use information from the text and your own experience to draw a conclusion that is not directly stated in the text, you are making an *inference*.

Below are five statements that may or may *not* be inferences based on the facts of the story. Write the letter *C* in the box in front of each statement that is a correct inference. Write the letter *F* in front of each faulty inference.

C—Correct Inference   F—Faulty Inference

____ ☐ 1. To have a good chance of winning the Iditarod, mushers and their dogs must be in good physical shape and get along well with each other.

____ ☐ 2. Large areas of Alaska have few, if any, settlers.

____ ☐ 3. Athletes who know how to swim and climb mountains have an advantage as mushers in the Iditarod.

____ ☐ 4. It is unlikely that huge numbers of spectators will ever line the Iditarod course, as they do at the Indy 500 or the Kentucky Derby.

____ ☐ 5. Competition between mushers is so fierce that each one is happy when storms, accidents, or other dangers cause problems for his or her rivals.

Score 5 points for each correct *C* or *F* answer.

____ TOTAL SCORE: Making Inferences

D USING WORDS PRECISELY

Each numbered sentence below contains an underlined word or phrase from the story you just read. Following the sentence are three definitions. One is a *synonym* for the underlined word, one is an *antonym*, and one has a completely *different* meaning than the underlined word.

For each definition, write the letter that stands for the correct answer in the box.

S—Synonym   A—Antonym   D—Different

1. There's only one thing they cannot be: cowards. If they are, they will never survive this <u>grueling</u> 1,160-mile race.
   ___ ☐ a. popular
   ___ ☐ b. very difficult
   ___ ☐ c. relaxed, easy-going

2. Hours later, after the snow finally stopped, Paulsen and the dogs dug themselves out. Then they <u>resumed</u> the race.
   ___ ☐ a. stopped altogether
   ___ ☐ b. watched
   ___ ☐ c. began again after an interruption

3. Some <u>exhausted</u> mushers begin to hallucinate.
   ___ ☐ a. extremely tired
   ___ ☐ b. fresh, full of energy
   ___ ☐ c. unfriendly

4. Some exhausted mushers begin to <u>hallucinate</u>.
   ___ ☐ a. speak loudly
   ___ ☐ b. face reality
   ___ ☐ c. have fantasies

5. Butcher tried to scare the moose off with an axe. But again and again, the animal tried to <u>trample</u> her dogs.
   ___ ☐ a. beat down with one's feet
   ___ ☐ b. gore
   ___ ☐ c. raise roughly

___ Score 3 points for a correct *S* answer.
___ Score 1 point for each correct *A* or *D* answer.

___ TOTAL SCORE: Using Words Precisely

• *Enter the total score for each exercise in the spaces below. Add the scores to find your Critical Reading Score. Then record your Critical Reading Score on the graph on page 114.*

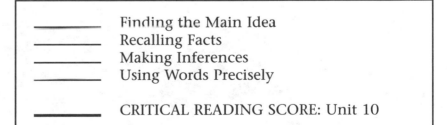

_____ Finding the Main Idea
_____ Recalling Facts
_____ Making Inferences
_____ Using Words Precisely

_____ CRITICAL READING SCORE: Unit 10

Group Three

Samuel Dixon walks a tightrope across the Niagara River in 1890. Dixon was one of many imitators of the most famous Niagara tightrope walker, Jean Francois Gravelet, know as Blondin. Blondin made his first walk in 1859. Besides walking ropes over the Niagara, daredevils have challenged the river by riding barrels over its falls.

CONQUERING NIAGARA FALLS

Most people go to Niagara Falls just to admire the view. They stand on the cliffs and gaze down at the 190-foot waterfalls. They may even shiver when they see the churning whirlpools at the bottom. Most visitors find this experience exciting enough.

A few people, however, want more. They want to challenge themselves. And so, over the years, daredevils have tried all kinds of loony stunts at Niagara Falls. They have tried swimming across the Falls. They have tried to steer a boat through the whirlpools. Some have even tumbled over the Falls in a giant rubber ball.

The madness began in 1859. An acrobat named Jean François Gravelet came to Niagara Falls. Called Blondin because of his blond hair, he decided he could make some money at the Falls. He arranged to have a cable strung across the river, about 190 feet above the water. On June 30 he prepared to walk from the American side of the Falls to the Canadian side. He would use no safety wire or net. All he wanted was his thirty-eight-pound balancing pole, which he would hold in his hands. When people heard of Blondin's plan, they flocked to the water's edge. They paid money to get a seat near the action.

As people held their breath, Blondin stepped onto the wire. Slowly he walked farther and farther out over the water. It was 1,200 feet to the other side. For seventeen and one-half minutes, Blondin carefully set one foot in front of the other. When he arrived on the far side, people went wild. Blondin became an instant hero.

From there, Blondin went on to even greater stunts. One day he pushed a wheelbarrow across the tightrope. On another occasion, he stopped and sipped champagne on the wire. There seemed to be no end to his daring antics. He did a headstand on the wire. He walked across it with baskets on his feet. He even made it across blindfolded.

Sometimes, though, things went wrong. One day Blondin carried a chair out over the Falls. He tried to balance the chair on two legs and then sit down on it. The chair wobbled. It fell into the swirling water below. For just a moment, Blondin lost his balance and nearly fell in after the chair.

Blondin's craziest stunt came on August 17. He tried to carry his manager across the Falls, piggy-back style. Halfway across, Blondin became tired. Winds kicked up, causing the tightrope to sway. Blondin had trouble moving forward. Sweat broke out on his face. At last, he stopped walking. He set his terrified manager down on the wire next to him. The two men rested for a few minutes. Then Blondin picked the manager up and started moving again. Several times Blondin had to stop and rest. At last he and the manager made it across, but it was a close call.

Blondin left Niagara Falls in 1860. But the idea of doing tricks there lingered on. In 1873 a French man named Ballini jumped 160 feet into the water below the Falls. Amazingly, he survived. In 1886 a Boston policeman named William J. Kendall decided to swim through the whirlpools. He, too, lived to tell about it. Meanwhile, Maria Spelterini followed Blondin's example. She crossed a tightrope over the Falls in 1876.

There was still one hurdle to be crossed. No one had ever traveled over the waterfall itself. Or, to be accurate, no one had ever traveled over the waterfall *and lived*. Schoolteacher Anna E. Taylor changed that in 1901. She survived the trip in a barrel. It was not a pleasant experience. By the time she climbed out of the barrel, her head was spinning. She was totally confused. "Did I go over the Falls yet?" she asked.

Later, Taylor warned people not to repeat her stunt. "If it was with my dying breath, I would caution anyone against attempting the feat," she said. Then she added, "I will never go over the Falls again. I would sooner walk up to the mouth of a cannon, knowing it was going to blow me to pieces, than make another trip over the Falls."

But some people didn't listen to Anna Taylor. They continued to flirt with death at Niagara Falls. Bobby Leach was one of those people. Leach ran a souvenir stand near the Falls. He bragged to customers about how easy it would be to take a barrel ride over the Falls. People asked him to prove it. And so in 1911, over he went. Leach made it, but he spent six months recuperating from the trip.

George Henry Stephen was not so lucky. In 1929 he died trying to go over the Falls. Reports indicated that his oak barrel was "smashed like an egg" by the pounding water. Rescuers saw his tattooed arm floating below the Falls. However, his body was never found.

Then there was George Stathakis. This Greek chef went over the Falls in a barrel made of wood and steel. The barrel held together during its plunge, but it became trapped in the whirlpools at the bottom of the Falls. For twenty-two hours, millions of tons of water crashed down on it. Sometime during those awful hours, Stathakis died.

Such deaths haven't stopped the thrill seekers, however. In 1985 John David Munday went over the Falls in a barrel. In 1993 he did it a second time. Munday used a homemade barrel with lots of padding. Even so, his body was cut and bruised during the trip. Rescuers found him passed out inside his barrel. Still, he survived. He became the first person to live through *two* trips over the Falls.

Spectators watch as a barrel carries a man down the Niagara.

Jessie Sharp wanted his name in the record books, too. He hoped to be the first person to go over the Falls in a canoe. Sharp made his attempt in 1990. He wore no helmet. He used no life jacket or other lifesaving equipment. Explained one friend, "Jessie felt he would stay with the boat. I think he really believed he would make it." Heading over the waterfall, Sharp raised his paddle in the air. Then he disappeared. After ten minutes, his paddle was seen floating at the bottom of the Falls. An hour later, his battered canoe was found. But Sharp himself was never seen again.

What's next? Who knows? But as long as water flows over Niagara Falls, it seems clear that daredevils will always find new ways to challenge themselves there.

If you have been timed while reading this selection, enter your reading time below. Then turn to the Words-per-Minute table on page 112 and look up your reading speed (words per minute). Enter your reading speed on the graph on page 113.

READING TIME: Unit 11	
_____ : _____	
Minutes	Seconds

How Well Did You Read?

- *Complete the four exercises that follow. The directions for each exercise will tell you how to mark your answers.*

- *When you have finished all four exercises, use the answer key on page 108 to check your work. For each right answer, put a check mark (✓) on the line beside the box. For each wrong answer, write the correct answer on the line.*

- *Follow the directions after each exercise to find your scores.*

 A **FINDING THE MAIN IDEA**

A good main idea statement answers two questions: it tells *who* or *what* is the subject of the story, and it answers the understood question *does what?* or *is what?* Look at the three statements below. One expresses the main idea of the story you just read. Another statement is *too broad*; it is vague and doesn't tell much about the topic of the story. The third statement is *too narrow*; it tells about only one part of the story.

Match the statements with the three answer choices below by writing the letter of each answer in the box in front of the statement it goes with.

M—Main Idea   **B—Too Broad**   **N—Too Narrow**

____ ☐ 1. Niagara Falls is a beautiful and powerful sight as well as a popular tourist attraction.

____ ☐ 2. Niagara Falls has been a magnet for daredevils for more than one hundred years.

____ ☐ 3. Acrobat Blondin's first trip across Niagara Falls on a tightrope took seventeen and one-half minutes.

____ Score 15 points for a correct *M* answer.
____ Score 5 points for each correct *B* or *N* answer.

____ TOTAL SCORE: Finding the Main Idea

B RECALLING FACTS

How well do you remember the facts in the story you just read? Put an *x* in the box in front of the correct answer to each of the multiple-choice questions below.

1. One feat that Blondin did NOT perform on the tightrope over Niagara Falls was
   - ___ ☐ a. doing a headstand.
   - ___ ☐ b. riding a bicycle.
   - ___ ☐ c. carrying another man on his back.

2. When Anna E. Taylor climbed out of the barrel, she
   - ___ ☐ a. was dizzy and confused.
   - ___ ☐ b. fired a cannon.
   - ___ ☐ c. said she wanted to try it again.

3. Before Bobby Leach went over the Falls, he had
   - ___ ☐ a. steered a boat through the whirlpools.
   - ___ ☐ b. jumped into the water below the Falls.
   - ___ ☐ c. run a souvenir stand near the Falls.

4. George Stathakis's trip over the Falls ended when
   - ___ ☐ a. the police stopped him from going over.
   - ___ ☐ b. his barrel became trapped in whirlpools.
   - ___ ☐ c. his barrel was crushed by the pounding water.

5. The only person who twice survived going over the Falls made his trips in a
   - ___ ☐ a. padded suit and helmet.
   - ___ ☐ b. giant rubber ball.
   - ___ ☐ c. padded barrel.

Score 5 points for each correct answer.

___ TOTAL SCORE: Recalling Facts

C MAKING INFERENCES

When you use information from the text and your own experience to draw a conclusion that is not directly stated in the text, you are making an *inference*.

Below are five statements that may or may *not* be inferences based on the facts of the story. Write the letter *C* in the box in front of each statement that is a correct inference. Write the letter *F* in front of each faulty inference.

C—Correct Inference   F—Faulty Inference

- ___ ☐ 1. Some people are willing to put themselves in danger just for excitement.

- ___ ☐ 2. Before 1901 no one ever thought of trying to go over Niagara Falls.

- ___ ☐ 3. If someone tried to walk a tightrope over Niagara Falls today, probably no one would bother to watch.

- ___ ☐ 4. In the last twenty years, it has become easier and less risky to travel over Niagara Falls.

- ___ ☐ 5. Whether you live or die, going over Niagara Falls is pretty much a matter of luck.

Score 5 points for each correct *C* or *F* answer.

___ TOTAL SCORE: Making Inferences

D USING WORDS PRECISELY

Each numbered sentence below contains an underlined word or phrase from the story you just read. Following the sentence are three definitions. One is a *synonym* for the underlined word, one is an *antonym*, and one has a completely *different* meaning than the underlined word.

For each definition, write the letter that stands for the correct answer in the box.

S—Synonym   A—Antonym   D—Different

1. They may even shiver when they see the <u>churning</u> whirlpools at the bottom.
   ___ a. wildly moving or shaking
   ___ b. magical
   ___ c. calm

2. And so, over the years, daredevils have tried all kinds of <u>loony</u> stunts at Niagara Falls.
   ___ a. sensible
   ___ b. foolish
   ___ c. expensive

3. Or, to be <u>accurate</u>, no one had ever traveled over the waterfall and lived.
   ___ a. wrong
   ___ b. kind
   ___ c. exactly correct

4. Leach made it, but he spent six months <u>recuperating</u> from the trip.
   ___ a. writing about experiences
   ___ b. returning to health
   ___ c. becoming worse

5. The barrel held together during its <u>plunge</u>, but it became trapped in the whirlpools at the bottom of the Falls.
   ___ a. sudden drop
   ___ b. upward movement
   ___ c. trick

___ Score 3 points for a correct *S* answer.
___ Score 1 point for each correct *A* or *D* answer.

___ TOTAL SCORE: Using Words Precisely

• *Enter the total score for each exercise in the spaces below. Add the scores to find your Critical Reading Score. Then record your Critical Reading Score on the graph on page 114.*

_____ Finding the Main Idea
_____ Recalling Facts
_____ Making Inferences
_____ Using Words Precisely

_____ CRITICAL READING SCORE: Unit 11

He's flying! And like any other pilot, Evel Knievel depended on the wind as well as his own skill. Conditions were right for Knievel on this jump over fourteen buses in 1975. This was his longest motorcycle jump to that date. Other successful stunts carried him into movies, songs, and international fame.

EVEL KNIEVEL: MOTORCYCLE MANIAC

Evel Knievel was doing "extreme sports" long before the term was even invented. He was a ski jumper, a sky diver, and a rodeo rider. But his real claim to fame came from jumping over things while riding on a motorcycle. His motorcycle stunts made him an American folk hero. Knievel started small but kept increasing the length of his jumps. Just how far would he go?

Knievel began doing his tricks in 1966. He drove his motorcycle through fire walls. He jumped over boxes of live snakes and landed between chained mountain lions. But his most popular stunt was jumping over cars. Knievel would ride his motorcycle up one ramp, fly over the cars, and land on another ramp on the other side. His first stunt jump was over two cars. Slowly, he worked his way up to sixteen cars.

Still, Knievel was really just a small-time stunt rider. All he got for risking life and limb was $500 a jump. But that changed on New Year's Day 1968. That's when he jumped 141 feet over a set of water fountains in front of a Las Vegas hotel. He made the

jump but crashed on the far side. He broke his pelvis bone and fractured his hip in several places. "I couldn't hang on to the motorcycle," he later said. "But, hey, I made the fountains."

The jump also made his reputation. Suddenly, Evel Knievel was the most famous stunt rider in the country. His fee soared to $7,500 a jump. Everyone recognized his white leather jacket with its red, white, and blue stars and stripes. Songs were written about him. In 1971 the movie *Evel Knievel* spread his fame even further.

Meanwhile, Knievel kept setting new records. In 1971 he cleared nineteen cars—a distance of 150 feet. Later, he cleared twenty cars. The landings were often smooth. But when they weren't—*ouch!* Knievel claimed that he had broken every bone in his body—except his neck. He was almost certainly right. Consider this: the human body has 206 bones. By the end of his career, Knievel had broken a total of 433 bones! He broke his arms so often that doctors had to put steel rods in them. His broken leg bones caused him to walk with a limp.

Still, Knievel healed fast and he

kept jumping. He was determined to live up to his image. His fans demanded longer and longer jumps. That meant he had to keep beating his own records. Knievel liked it that way. As he put it, "I want it so that when . . . [people] look at that jump and . . . see how far it is, [they're] going to say, 'No *way*. There's just no way he can make it. He's a dead duck.'"

Knievel wanted not only to amaze his fans but also to please them. He felt he shared a special bond with them. As he said, "When [they] see me make the practice runs, getting ready . . . , [they] are just as scared as I am. When I make it, [they] are just as glad."

And so his stunts became wilder and wilder. In 1974 Knievel took on the ultimate challenge. He agreed to jump the Snake River Canyon in Twin Falls, Idaho. The canyon was a mile wide! Knievel planned to use his Sky-Cycle X-2 to make the jump. The Sky-Cycle was not a real motorcycle. It was a special steam-powered rocket built to go 350 miles per hour. It would shoot Knievel 2,000 feet up and, he hoped, over the canyon. For this stunt he was guaranteed $6 million!

To promote the jump, Knievel toured the nation. He visited thirty-nine cities in twelve days. He called it Evel Knievel's Goodbye Tour. What kind of a goodbye was he talking about? Knievel said he meant that he would retire after the jump—if he lived. So the "goodbye" could work two ways.

The stunt captured the imagination of the country. Some people thought he was a hero. Others thought he was a clown. Still others thought he was a lunatic. At times, even Knievel didn't know what he was. "I don't know if I'm an athlete, a daredevil, a hoax, or a nut," he said before the jump. In any event, he knew what *might* happen. "I'll be competing against the toughest opponent of all. And that's death."

On September 8, 1974, the day of the jump, all the talk came to an end. Knievel knew it was time for action. Things didn't look good. The winds were tricky and the Sky-Cycle was untested. Robert Truax, Knievel's own adviser, said that his chances were no better than fifty-fifty. Still, there was no turning back. So Knievel climbed into the Sky-Cycle and strapped himself in.

The Sky-Cycle surged up the ramp. And then the jump fizzled. Somehow the Sky-Cycle's two parachutes opened far too soon. (They were not supposed to open until Knievel reached the far side of the canyon.) So the Sky-Cycle didn't roar over the Snake River Canyon. Instead, it skimmed down the near side of the canyon, bouncing off some rocks as it fell. Then Knievel and his Sky-Cycle came to rest in some trees.

After the Sky-Cycle flop, Knievel did not retire. He went on jumping over things—and he went on breaking bones. In 1975 he broke his pelvis (again) and both hands. He crashed after leaping over thirteen double-decker buses in London, England.

At long last, in 1981, Evel Knievel called it quits. He had been defying death for fifteen years. But he could no longer keep up with the demands of his fans. "I can't live up to the image people have of me," he said. "Every time they see a canyon, they think I ought to jump over it." No more. The great motorcycle stunt rider had made his last jump and broken his last bone.

If you have been timed while reading this selection, enter your reading time below. Then turn to the Words-per-Minute table on page 112 and look up your reading speed (words per minute). Enter your reading speed on the graph on page 113.

READING TIME: Unit 12	
_____ : _____	
Minutes	*Seconds*

How Well Did You Read?

- *Complete the four exercises that follow. The directions for each exercise will tell you how to mark your answers.*

- *When you have finished all four exercises, use the answer key on page 108 to check your work. For each right answer, put a check mark (✓) on the line beside the box. For each wrong answer, write the correct answer on the line.*

- *Follow the directions after each exercise to find your scores.*

 **FINDING THE MAIN IDEA**

A good main idea statement answers two questions: it tells *who* or *what* is the subject of the story, and it answers the understood question *does what?* or *is what?* Look at the three statements below. One expresses the main idea of the story you just read. Another statement is *too broad*; it is vague and doesn't tell much about the topic of the story. The third statement is *too narrow*; it tells about only one part of the story.

Match the statements with the three answer choices below by writing the letter of each answer in the box in front of the statement it goes with.

M—Main Idea **B—Too Broad** **N—Too Narrow**

_____ ☐ 1. When Evel Knievel began his career, all he got for risking his life in motorcycle jumps was $500.

_____ ☐ 2. Jumping over cars is a dangerous stunt that only the most skilled riders should attempt.

_____ ☐ 3. Evel Knievel, motorcycle stunt man, amazed the public for years with his daredevil jumps.

_____ Score 15 points for a correct *M* answer.
_____ Score 5 points for each correct *B* or *N* answer.

_____ TOTAL SCORE: Finding the Main Idea

B RECALLING FACTS

How well do you remember the facts in the story you just read? Put an *x* in the box in front of the correct answer to each of the multiple-choice questions below.

1. On his longest jump, Evel Knievel cleared
   - ☐ a. twenty cars.
   - ☐ b. sixteen cars.
   - ☐ c. thirteen cars.

2. The jump that made Knievel's reputation took place over a set of water fountains in
   - ☐ a. Los Angeles.
   - ☐ b. Las Vegas.
   - ☐ c. Idaho.

3. Knievel's Sky-Cycle was a
   - ☐ a. regular motorcycle.
   - ☐ b. steam-powered rocket.
   - ☐ c. type of airplane.

4. The jump over Snake River fizzled because
   - ☐ a. the Sky-Cycle would not start.
   - ☐ b. Knievel backed out at the last minute.
   - ☐ c. the parachutes opened too quickly.

5. In 1975, Knievel jumped over
   - ☐ a. thirteen double-decker buses in London.
   - ☐ b. the Snake River Canyon.
   - ☐ c. twenty-two cars.

Score 5 points for each correct answer.

____ TOTAL SCORE: Recalling Facts

C MAKING INFERENCES

When you use information from the text and your own experience to draw a conclusion that is not directly stated in the text, you are making an *inference*.

Below are five statements that may or may *not* be inferences based on the facts of the story. Write the letter *C* in the box in front of each statement that is a correct inference. Write the letter *F* in front of each faulty inference.

C—Correct Inference   F—Faulty Inference

1. Trying to jump over canyons in Idaho was probably illegal in 1974.

2. Knievel was willing to accept damage to his body in exchange for the thrill of jumping.

3. The weather may have had an effect on the outcome of the Sky-Cycle jump.

4. Knievel tried to jump the Snake River Canyon using the Sky-Cycle because he thought it would be impossible with a regular motorcycle.

5. Knievel was a popular performer only in the United States.

Score 5 points for each correct *C* or *F* answer.

____ TOTAL SCORE: Making Inferences

USING WORDS PRECISELY

Each numbered sentence below contains an underlined word or phrase from the story you just read. Following the sentence are three definitions. One is a *synonym* for the underlined word, one is an *antonym*, and one has a completely *different* meaning than the underlined word.

For each definition, write the letter that stands for the correct answer in the box.

S—Synonym   A—Antonym   D—Different

1. His fee <u>soared</u> to $7,500 a jump.
   ___ ☐ a. fell
   ___ ☐ b. changed
   ___ ☐ c. rose

2. In 1971 he <u>cleared</u> nineteen cars—a distance of 150 feet.
   ___ ☐ a. went over or by without touching
   ___ ☐ b. crashed into
   ___ ☐ c. moved

3. <u>Consider</u> this: the human body has 206 bones.
   ___ ☐ a. ignore
   ___ ☐ b. play
   ___ ☐ c. think about

4. Still others thought he was a <u>lunatic</u>.
   ___ ☐ a. sensible person
   ___ ☐ b. person who is crazy
   ___ ☐ c. hero

5. In 1974 he took on the <u>ultimate</u> challenge.
   ___ ☐ a. greatest
   ___ ☐ b. dangerous
   ___ ☐ c. smallest or least

___ Score 3 points for a correct *S* answer.
___ Score 1 point for each correct *A* or *D* answer.

___ TOTAL SCORE: Using Words Precisely

• *Enter the total score for each exercise in the spaces below. Add the scores to find your Critical Reading Score. Then record your Critical Reading Score on the graph on page 114.*

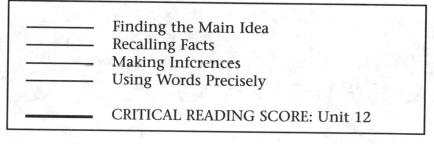

_____ Finding the Main Idea
_____ Recalling Facts
_____ Making Inferences
_____ Using Words Precisely

_____ CRITICAL READING SCORE: Unit 12

Lucky and skillful players among the hundreds on the buzkashi field close in on the spot where the buz—the body of a goat—lies. The men are intent on finding the buz in the cloud of dust. Whoever gets close enough will reach down, grab the heavy body, and try to carry it across the field at a gallop.

BUZKASHI: WAR ON HORSEBACK

What is Afghanistan's national sport? If you guessed soccer, wrestling, or any other common activity, you're wrong. In Afghanistan the national sport is no ordinary game. The name itself should give you a clue. It is *buzkashi*, which means "goat grabbing."

Buzkashi has a long history. It began nearly eight hundred years ago. That was when a famous Afghan leader named Genghis Khan led an army of soldiers on horseback. Khan and his men conquered lands from China to Europe. Khan's soldiers were the finest horsemen in the world. They could mount at a moment's notice. They could ride all day. These brutal warriors could attack and fight without ever getting off their horses.

To keep their riding skills sharp, the horsemen played a special game. They tried to scoop up an object while riding a horse at high speeds. In those days, the object they grabbed was the body of a dead enemy. Today, a human corpse is no longer used. But the game lives on. The only difference is that now buzkashi players use the headless body of a goat.

Before the game begins, the players mount their horses. There are usually two or three teams made up of several horsemen each. The total number of players can range from about ten to a hundred. The object of the game is pretty simple. The goat, called the *buz*, is put into a ditch. On a given signal—often a rifle shot or a whistle—all the horsemen rush to the ditch. Each one tries to grab the goat and lift it onto his saddle.

The one who gets the goat races off. With one hand grasping the goat and the other handling the reins, this horseman may end up holding his whip between his teeth. He tries to gallop down the field, around a pole, and back to the ditch, where he then drops the goat. If he manages to do all this, his team scores a point.

Right from the beginning, the riders on the other teams try to wrestle the buz away from him. They'll do whatever it takes to get that goat. The results are often violent. Riders and horses get knocked all over the place. Even the horses kick and bite each other. The fighting for the buz is so fierce that the body of the

goat may get torn to pieces. If that happens, another one is brought out to replace it.

In his book *The Horsemen*, Joseph Kessel describes the start of one game. "Silently, step by step, the sixty horsemen [surround] the hole that [holds] the slaughtered beast." The players, wearing team colors, form a circle. Then the horses explode toward each other. Kessel writes that the field turns into "an enormous whirlwind." The air is filled with "whoops, oaths, wordless threats, . . . lashing whips ripping into muzzles and faces." The riders fight as if their lives depend on it. They struggle with "their faces in the dust, their nails clawing . . . to find the headless goat, grasp it, and snatch it up."

At times there is nothing to see but a huge cloud of dust. Then, suddenly, one rider emerges with the buz. A second later, the others are charging after him. If they catch him, the battle for the goat begins anew.

When a point is finally scored, there is a break in the game. Money or gifts are awarded to the winning rider. The contest usually doesn't end until all the prize money and gifts have been given out. So some games last all day.

To be successful, players need good horses. Horses are bred especially to play buzkashi, and good ones cost a lot of money. When a buzkashi colt is born, its feet are not allowed to touch the ground. According to an Afghan tradition, touching the earth too soon would cause the colt to lose its "wings." Later, the young colts are trained to dodge and attack at the rider's command. They are also trained not to step on a fallen rider. That explains how such a rough sport can have so few serious injuries.

The Afghans love their buzkashi horses. They will spend years training them. The best ones last up to twenty years as buzkashi mounts. In fact, many people in Afghanistan regard the horses more highly than the riders. They often say, "Better to have a poor rider on a good horse than a good rider on a poor horse."

Best of all, of course, is to have both a good horse *and* a good rider. It takes a long, long time to become a top rider. Young boys spend years training in their villages. They must develop incredible balance and a keen sense of timing. In addition, they must be very strong, since the buz alone often weighs close to a hundred pounds. Most riders don't reach the top of their game until they are in their late thirties or early forties.

Buzkashi is a serious sport. It isn't the kind of contest where you shake hands at the end. There is too much pride involved. And if winning brings pride, losing brings shame. One Afghan said, "It is better to shoot a [man] with a gun straight in the face than to tell him loudly on the buzkashi field that his horse is weak and not fast enough."

In 1955 Afghanistan made buzkashi an official sport. That meant setting some clear-cut rules. These rules cover such things as the shape of the field, scoring, and the size of the teams. The rules provide for a regular season with playoffs and a championship. The rules also try to tone down the violence. Mounted referees can call two kinds of fouls. One is for whipping a player on purpose. The other is for pulling a rider off his horse.

Buzkashi, however, is too important to be played only by the best players. Anyone can set up a match. All you need is someone who can offer money or prizes. So unofficial games are still played all the time. And they are played the old-fashioned way—war on horseback with no rules.

If you have been timed while reading this selection, enter your reading time below. Then turn to the Words-per-Minute table on page 112 and look up your reading speed (words per minute). Enter your reading speed on the graph on page 113.

READING TIME: Unit 13

_____ : _____

Minutes   *Seconds*

How Well Did You Read?

- *Complete the four exercises that follow. The directions for each exercise will tell you how to mark your answers.*

- *When you have finished all four exercises, use the answer key on page 108 to check your work. For each right answer, put a check mark (✓) on the line beside the box. For each wrong answer, write the correct answer on the line.*

- *Follow the directions after each exercise to find your scores.*

 FINDING THE MAIN IDEA

A good main idea statement answers two questions: it tells *who* or *what* is the subject of the story, and it answers the understood question *does what?* or *is what?* Look at the three statements below. One expresses the main idea of the story you just read. Another statement is *too broad*; it is vague and doesn't tell much about the topic of the story. The third statement is *too narrow*; it tells about only one part of the story.

Match the statements with the three answer choices below by writing the letter of each answer in the box in front of the statement it goes with.

M—Main Idea   B—Too Broad   N—Too Narrow

____ ☐ 1. In the warlike game of buzkashi, teams of men on horseback struggle with each other to pick up the body of a goat and carry it across a field.

____ ☐ 2. Afghanistan's national sport, buzkashi, or "goat grabbing," is no ordinary game.

____ ☐ 3. The goat's body used in Afghanistan's buzkashi game replaces the human body used by Genghis Khan's warriors.

____ Score 15 points for a correct *M* answer.
____ Score 5 points for each correct *B* or *N* answer.

____ TOTAL SCORE: Finding the Main Idea

B RECALLING FACTS

How well do you remember the facts in the story you just read? Put an *x* in the box in front of the correct answer to each of the multiple-choice questions below.

1. Buzkashi began nearly eight hundred years ago when
   ____ ☐ a. the game became Afghanistan's national sport.
   ____ ☐ b. Genghis Khan's warriors were conquering lands from China to Europe.
   ____ ☐ c. Afghanistan took on its modern borders.

2. Centuries ago, warriors played buzkashi
   ____ ☐ a. to relax after a hard day of fighting.
   ____ ☐ b. to win money in professional competitions.
   ____ ☐ c. to keep their fighting and riding skills sharp.

3. The number of players on the field at once
   ____ ☐ a. is limited to ten.
   ____ ☐ b. is never over fifty.
   ____ ☐ c. may range up to a hundred or so.

4. As play begins, every horseman tries to
   ____ ☐ a. pick up the headless body of a goat.
   ____ ☐ b. show how fast he can ride straight ahead.
   ____ ☐ c. get the attention of the spectators.

5. The horses ridden in a buzkashi game are
   ____ ☐ a. assigned to riders by a lottery.
   ____ ☐ b. well trained and quick to react.
   ____ ☐ c. usually worn out after two years or so.

Score 5 points for each correct answer.

____ TOTAL SCORE: Recalling Facts

C MAKING INFERENCES

When you use information from the text and your own experience to draw a conclusion that is not directly stated in the text, you are making an *inference*.

Below are five statements that may or may *not* be inferences based on the facts of the story. Write the letter *C* in the box in front of each statement that is a correct inference. Write the letter *F* in front of each faulty inference.

C—Correct Inference   F—Faulty Inference

____ ☐ 1. Many people in Afghanistan live in the country or in villages where they can own horses.

____ ☐ 2. Buzkashi did not have clear-cut, official rules before 1955.

____ ☐ 3. The man who first picks up the goat's body is usually the one who scores a point.

____ ☐ 4. A buzkashi rider must pay a great deal for a horse that is good in buzkashi.

____ ☐ 5. A buzkashi player would consider the American game of professional football as overly rough.

Score 5 points for each correct *C* or *F* answer.

____ TOTAL SCORE: Making Inferences

Each numbered sentence below contains an underlined word or phrase from the story you just read. Following the sentence are three definitions. One is a *synonym* for the underlined word, one is an *antonym*, and one has a completely *different* meaning than the underlined word.

For each definition, write the letter that stands for the correct answer in the box.

S—Synonym   A—Antonym   D—Different

1. Khan and his men <u>conquered</u> lands from China to Europe.

____ ☐ a. visited

____ ☐ b. took by force

____ ☐ c. gave up

2. They tried to <u>scoop up</u> an object while riding a horse at high speeds.

____ ☐ a. set loose, drop

____ ☐ b. identify

____ ☐ c. gather up swiftly, grab

3. Silently, step by step, the sixty horsemen [surround] the hole that [holds] the <u>slaughtered</u> beast.

____ ☐ a. butchered

____ ☐ b. hidden

____ ☐ c. revived, restored

4. At times there is nothing to see but a huge cloud of dust. Then, suddenly, one rider <u>emerges</u> with the buz.

____ ☐ a. stands

____ ☐ b. comes out

____ ☐ c. goes in

5. Young boys spend years training in their villages. They must develop <u>incredible</u> balance and a keen sense of timing.

____ ☐ a. extraordinary

____ ☐ b. barely adequate

____ ☐ c. changeable

____ Score 3 points for a correct *S* answer.
____ Score 1 point for each correct *A* or *D* answer.

____ TOTAL SCORE: Using Words Precisely

• *Enter the total score for each exercise in the spaces below. Add the scores to find your Critical Reading Score. Then record your Critical Reading Score on the graph on page 114.*

_____ Finding the Main Idea
_____ Recalling Facts
_____ Making Inferences
_____ Using Words Precisely

_____ CRITICAL READING SCORE: Unit 13

You're watching a crime in progress. Jumping off Buildings, Antennae, bridge Spans, and Earthbound objects–also known as BASE jumping–is illegal throughout the United States. Even so, some extreme sportspeople consider the legal risks part of the sport, just as the risks of injury and death are. These BASE jumpers are leaping off buildings in downtown Los Angeles. Once they land, they could be arrested.

BASE JUMPING: THE OUTER EDGE OF DANGER

On October 18, 1990, a young man walked into St. Paul's Cathedral in London, England. He began to climb the stairs to the Whispering Gallery that stands 102 feet above the cathedral floor. No one paid any attention to this man or to the friend who was with him. No one noticed the parachute the man wore on his back.

Soon the young man reached the gallery. He climbed over the safety railing. Then, to the astonishment of everyone in the church, he jumped. The friend who was with him stayed in the gallery and pulled the rip cord on the parachute. (The jumper wouldn't have had time to open it himself.) As the man floated to the floor, he almost hit a woman. He landed, then scrambled out of his parachute and ran away before police could arrest him.

The unknown man was a BASE jumper. That's someone who parachutes from a low level. The term *BASE* refers to the objects such a person jumps from: *B*uildings, *A*ntennae, bridge *S*pans, and other *E*arthbound objects. More and more people are taking up this sport. They are parachuting off cliffs, towers, bridges—and just about anything else that juts up into the air.

BASE jumping is far more risky than normal parachuting. First, there is the danger of smacking into the side of the object from which you have jumped. Second, when you jump from a plane there is lots of time to open your parachute. But when you jump from a building or cliff, you have just a few seconds.

Finally, when you jump from a plane you have *two* parachutes. If the first one doesn't open, you still have another one to try. In BASE jumping you don't have enough time to open a second chute. So there's no point in wearing one. If the one chute you have doesn't work, that's all there is to it. On the plus side, at least you don't have long to worry about what's ahead!

For most people, regular parachuting is an extreme sport. So, too, is mountain biking and high-speed inline skating. But these sports don't cut it any more with BASE jumpers. In their opinion, the risk of a bloody nose or a scraped knee isn't enough to make a sport "extreme." For BASE jumpers, there has to be a real chance that you'll die. As BASE jumper Mike Steele said, "We have redefined what makes for a daring and dangerous adventure. Now it takes more effort to be extreme."

So BASE jumpers look for wild places from which to leap. One popular spot is Angel Falls in Venezuela. At 3,212 feet, it is the highest waterfall in the world. Jan Davis, a grandmother, once jumped there. The fact that she could have been mangled or killed didn't seem to bother her. "I have nothing to prove to anyone," she said. "I do it because I enjoy it."

More than thirty BASE jumpers have died since the sport began. In fact, the sport is so dangerous it is banned throughout the United States. Exceptions are granted only for a few special occasions. Still, people break the law and keep BASE jumping anyway. "It's definitely an underground thing," said one BASE jumper. "You get in so much trouble for even thinking about doing it."

The Royal Gorge Bridge in Colorado is 1,053 feet high. It is the highest suspension bridge in the world. That makes it an attraction for BASE jumpers. A Colorado state law prohibits people from jumping off the bridge. But every year, two or three people try it. "We catch some; some get away," said police lieutenant Steve McLaury.

Donald Samson knew it was illegal. Still, in 1994 he decided to jump off the Royal Gorge Bridge. Something went terribly wrong with Samson's leap. He died from severe head injuries. The police don't know for sure what went wrong. Lieutenant McLaury suggested that Samson might have been caught in a wind shift. That could have caused him to slam into the rocks on the way down. Maybe he didn't open his chute fast enough. Or perhaps the chute itself didn't work properly. In any case, at the age of twenty-six, Donald Samson joined the ranks of dead BASE jumpers.

Alf Humphries was forty-nine when he made his last jump. Humphries had plenty of experience. He had skydived more than 2,800 times. He had BASE jumped 130 times, including a leap off the Royal Gorge Bridge. Humphries had even plunged off the roofs of office buildings in Los Angeles and Denver.

In 1993 Humphries tried an "easy" jump off a 950-foot tower in Colorado. But nothing about BASE jumping is easy. Humphries understood that. Some of his friends had been badly injured BASE jumping. Humphries himself had broken his knees, legs, ankles, and feet. But this time it was much worse. His parachute didn't open all the way. It slowed him down enough so that he wasn't killed. But Humphries hit the ground so hard he broke his spine. As a result, he will spend the rest of his life in a wheelchair.

Humphries now wishes he hadn't taken up BASE jumping. He advises others not to do it. As Humphries said, "Life is not as much fun as it was." But others continue to jump, regardless of the risks. As Scott Chew, a friend of Humphries, said, "[BASE jumping] is just like any other sport. People don't stop riding bicycles just because they read about other people falling off bicycles." On the other hand, when someone falls off a bicycle, people don't talk about outlawing the sport. And they usually don't need to bury the biker.

If you have been timed while reading this selection, enter your reading time below. Then turn to the Words-per-Minute table on page 112 and look up your reading speed (words per minute). Enter your reading speed on the graph on page 113.

| **READING TIME: Unit 14** |
| _____ : _____ |
| *Minutes* *Seconds* |

How Well Did You Read?

- *Complete the four exercises that follow. The directions for each exercise will tell you how to mark your answers.*

- *When you have finished all four exercises, use the answer key on page 108 to check your work. For each right answer, put a check mark (✓) on the line beside the box. For each wrong answer, write the correct answer on the line.*

- *Follow the directions after each exercise to find your scores.*

A FINDING THE MAIN IDEA

A good main idea statement answers two questions: it tells *who* or *what* is the subject of the story, and it answers the understood question *does what?* or *is what?* Look at the three statements below. One expresses the main idea of the story you just read. Another statement is *too broad*; it is vague and doesn't tell much about the topic of the story. The third statement is *too narrow*; it tells about only one part of the story.

Match the statements with the three answer choices below by writing the letter of each answer in the box in front of the statement it goes with.

M—Main Idea   **B—Too Broad**   **N—Too Narrow**

____ ☐ 1. A BASE jumper uses only one parachute since there isn't enough time to try a second one.

____ ☐ 2. BASE jumping is a dangerous way to get a thrill, as proved by the number of people who have been injured or even killed while attempting it.

____ ☐ 3. BASE jumping is a popular extreme sport in many parts of the world.

____ Score 15 points for a correct *M* answer.
____ Score 5 points for each correct *B* or *N* answer.

____ TOTAL SCORE: Finding the Main Idea

RECALLING FACTS

How well do you remember the facts in the story you just read? Put an *x* in the box in front of the correct answer to each of the multiple-choice questions below.

1. The BASE jumper at St. Paul's Cathedral
   ____ ☐ a. was immediately arrested.
   ____ ☐ b. was taken to the nearest hospital.
   ____ ☐ c. ran away before the police arrived.

2. Every BASE jumper needs
   ____ ☐ a. a parachute.
   ____ ☐ b. a life jacket.
   ____ ☐ c. special shoes.

3. Jumping from the following place would NOT be called BASE jumping:
   ____ ☐ a. the Empire State Building.
   ____ ☐ b. a helicopter.
   ____ ☐ c. a radio station antenna.

4. The highest waterfall in the world is
   ____ ☐ a. Victoria Falls in Africa.
   ____ ☐ b. Niagara Falls between the U.S. and Canada.
   ____ ☐ c. Angel Falls in Venezuela.

5. Alf Humphries's parachute caused his accident by
   ____ ☐ a. not opening all the way.
   ____ ☐ b. opening too soon.
   ____ ☐ c. failing to open at all.

Score 5 points for each correct answer.

____ TOTAL SCORE: Recalling Facts

C **MAKING INFERENCES**

When you use information from the text and your own experience to draw a conclusion that is not directly stated in the text, you are making an *inference*.

Below are five statements that may or may *not* be inferences based on the facts of the story. Write the letter *C* in the box in front of each statement that is a correct inference. Write the letter *F* in front of each faulty inference.

C—Correct Inference   F—Faulty Inference

____ ☐ 1. BASE jumpers who jump off the Royal Gorge Bridge do not have much respect for the laws of Colorado.

____ ☐ 2. A truly skilled BASE jumper probably doesn't need a friend or partner nearby.

____ ☐ 3. The U.S. government tries to protect its citizens, even from themselves.

____ ☐ 4. If police find out about an accident in which someone dies, they usually investigate its causes.

____ ☐ 5. If you are an experienced BASE jumper, you can be sure that your next jump will be successful and safe.

Score 5 points for each correct *C* or *F* answer.

____ TOTAL SCORE: Making Inferences

D USING WORDS PRECISELY

Each numbered sentence below contains an underlined word or phrase from the story you just read. Following the sentence are three definitions. One is a *synonym* for the underlined word, one is an *antonym*, and one has a completely *different* meaning than the underlined word.

For each definition, write the letter that stands for the correct answer in the box.

S—Synonym   A—Antonym   D—Different

1. Then, to the underline astonishment of everyone in the church, he jumped.

   ____ ☐ a. indifference

   ____ ☐ b. surprise

   ____ ☐ c. applause

2. The term *BASE* refers to the objects these people jump from: *Buildings, Antennae,* bridge *Spans,* and other underline Earthbound objects.

   ____ ☐ a. floating in space

   ____ ☐ b. tall

   ____ ☐ c. located on or held to the earth

3. In fact, the sport is so dangerous it is underline banned throughout the United States.

   ____ ☐ a. forbidden

   ____ ☐ b. talked about

   ____ ☐ c. encouraged

4. It's definitely an underline underground thing.

   ____ ☐ a. frightening

   ____ ☐ b. open and obvious

   ____ ☐ c. secret or hidden

5. In their opinion, the risk of a bloody nose or a scraped knee isn't enough to make a sport "underline extreme."

   ____ ☐ a. extraordinary

   ____ ☐ b. normal

   ____ ☐ c. fun

____ Score 3 points for a correct *S* answer.
____ Score 1 point for each correct *A* or *D* answer.

____ TOTAL SCORE: Using Words Precisely

• *Enter the total score for each exercise in the spaces below. Add the scores to find your Critical Reading Score. Then record your Critical Reading Score on the graph on page 114.*

____ Finding the Main Idea
____ Recalling Facts
____ Making Inferences
____ Using Words Precisely

____ CRITICAL READING SCORE: Unit 14

Contestants in the Raid Gauloises must be ready for anything! These photos are from the 1995 Raid, which was held in Patagonia, Argentina. The team at the left is descending from Mount Tronador on the second leg of the race. The team shown above rides on horseback through the Pampas Lindas on the fourth leg.

RAID GAULOISES: TEN DAYS OF HELL

First you are climbing the walls of a huge canyon as water from a waterfall pounds on your head. Then you are kayaking through shark-filled waters with a storm raging all around you. Next you are riding a camel across a desert with sand blowing in your face and the sun beating down on your back. Are you trapped in some kind of bad dream? No, but that's close. You are in the Raid Gauloises, a grueling ten-day race that takes people to the edge of death.

The Raid Gauloises (pronounced *rād gōl•wahz*) started in 1989. A Frenchman named Gérard Fusil set it up. Fusil wanted a race that would lead people through the wildest lands left on earth. He wanted racers to stretch themselves beyond all human limits. He wanted them to cover huge distances and face many dangers. In return, winners would receive thousands of dollars in prize money. But more than that, they would have the joy of knowing they survived the toughest course Mother Nature could offer.

Fusil set up simple rules for the race. Athletes must compete in groups of five. At least one person in each group must be a woman. And, in order to win, the entire team has to make it to the finish line. If one person drops out, the whole team is disqualified.

Teams have ten days to complete five legs, or stages, of the race. Each leg requires different skills. One leg might involve rock climbing. Another might include parachuting off a mountaintop. A third might call for whitewater rafting, long-distance running, or mountain biking.

To keep the race fresh, Fusil decided it should be held in a different place each year. Racers are told the general location months in advance. But they don't know the exact route until twenty-four hours before race time. Then they are given maps showing the starting and finish lines of each leg. The maps also show the checkpoints the teams must pass through. Otherwise, the course is not marked. There are no aid stations along the way and no trails to follow. So each team is truly on its own. The only help comes in the form of rescue helicopters. Teams carry flares that they can shoot off if they want a helicopter to come get them. But since that means dropping out of the race, flares are always a last resort.

In 1990 the Raid Gauloises was held in Costa Rica. Athletes had to race through jungles thick with poisonous snakes. They had to hike miles through alligator country. They had to contend with sweltering heat, endless beds of loose sand, and the constant threat of panther attacks.

In 1992 the race was set in the Arab country of Oman. Here, athletes had to watch out for scorpions. They had to deal with jellyfish and leeches. They ran the risk of getting malaria and heatstroke. The 1994 race took place in Borneo. The jungles were so thick that it was hard to get through them. One U.S. team got lost in the tangled overgrowth. The team wandered for twenty-four hours before finally finding its way out.

Despite the punishing nature of the race, it is a big success. In 1995 forty-eight teams from around the world came to compete in it. This time the setting was Patagonia, an area of southern Argentina. As always,

"Raiders" were warned of the problems they would face. The temperature could range from 20 to 110 degrees Fahrenheit. There would be snow in the mountains and ice in the lakes. Yet during the day, the sun would be very hot. Athletes were urged to use their sunscreen, even on their lips. Otherwise, said one race official, "your lips will swell up like huge tomatoes."

When the race began, the teams took off across a lake in sea kayaks. They had to paddle thirty-one miles in strong winds. Everyone made it through this first leg. But the second leg was harder. The athletes had to climb up a huge, jagged mountain called Mount Tronador. The sun beat down without mercy. One woman became sick and couldn't stop vomiting. One climber hurt his knee and saw it puff up to the size of a grapefruit. Meanwhile, a French team got lost. They spent nine hours struggling to get back on course.

As the hours slipped by, all the Raiders grew weary. Yet they were reluctant to stop. They knew that each minute they rested, they were losing ground to some other team. Besides, the idea of camping in the snow without sleeping bags was not very appealing. On the other hand, climbing in the dark was no picnic, either. One woman broke her leg doing that. Another man's hand was crushed by a rock that fell in the dark.

Those who kept going eventually found themselves surrounded by ice. To get to the top of Mount Tronador, the members of each team had to rope themselves together. That was the only way to be sure they didn't slip off, fall off, or blow off the mountain.

By this time, the athletes were in their fourth full day of racing. They were exhausted. They staggered along with their backs bent and their eyes sunk in. Some had frostbite on their feet. One man started hallucinating. Another developed pneumonia. Many were badly burned by the sun. Writer David Tracey, who followed the progress of the athletes, noted that "one [American] racer . . . is suffering from a sunburned tongue. He does not want to talk about it."

By the end of the mountain stage, more than ten teams had dropped out. The rest were struggling to hang on. "This mountain made me cry," said French Raider Isabelle Mir as she came down off Mount Tronador. "I've never suffered so much physically and mentally." Yet she and many others pushed on to the canoeing stage. Here, teams had to fight their way through whitewater rapids. In places, they had to leave the water and carry their canoes for miles through bamboo forests. A Spanish team, made up of all women, finished this bruising forty-mile leg in just thirty hours. They did it without taking a single break along the way.

The fourth stage required teams to complete a long, hard ride on horseback. Several riders were thrown from their horses, but they climbed back on and kept going. The final stage was a walk-run-climb through canyons and forests. An Austrian team lost its map in this section. They began to wander around in desperation. Luckily, they found a French team that offered to share its map with them.

Many people might think those who compete in the Raid Gauloises are just plain nuts. But don't try to tell that to the athletes who have done it. For them, Raid Gauloises is the ultimate challenge in the world of sports.

If you have been timed while reading this selection, enter your reading time below. Then turn to the Words-per-Minute table on page 112 and look up your reading speed (words per minute). Enter your reading speed on the graph on page 113.

READING TIME: Unit 15	
_____ : _____	
Minutes	*Seconds*

How Well Did You Read?

- *Complete the four exercises that follow. The directions for each exercise will tell you how to mark your answers.*

- *When you have finished all four exercises, use the answer key on page 108 to check your work. For each right answer, put a check mark (✓) on the line beside the box. For each wrong answer, write the correct answer on the line.*

- *Follow the directions after each exercise to find your scores.*

 FINDING THE MAIN IDEA

A good main idea statement answers two questions: it tells *who* or *what* is the subject of the story, and it answers the understood question *does what?* or *is what?* Look at the three statements below. One expresses the main idea of the story you just read. Another statement is *too broad*; it is vague and doesn't tell much about the topic of the story. The third statement is *too narrow*; it tells about only one part of the story.

Match the statements with the three answer choices below by writing the letter of each answer in the box in front of the statement it goes with.

M—Main Idea   **B—Too Broad**   **N—Too Narrow**

____ ☐   1. The Raid Gauloises was started in 1989 by a Frenchman named Gérard Fusil.

____ ☐   2. Perhaps the most extreme of extreme sports is the Raid Gauloises.

____ ☐   3. The Raid Gauloises, a ten-day race held each year in wild lands, tests athletes under the worst conditions.

____   Score 15 points for a correct *M* answer.
____   Score 5 points for each correct *B* or *N* answer.

____   TOTAL SCORE: Finding the Main Idea

B RECALLING FACTS

How well do you remember the facts in the story you just read? Put an *x* in the box in front of the correct answer to each of the multiple-choice questions below.

1. Each five-member team must include at least
   - ☐ a. one woman.
   - ☐ b. one French person.
   - ☐ c. one professional athlete.

2. If one member of a team drops out,
   - ☐ a. the team uses a flare to notify officials.
   - ☐ b. the rest of the team must call in a substitute.
   - ☐ c. the whole team is disqualified.

3. The teams are guided through the course by
   - ☐ a. signs and guideposts spaced one mile apart.
   - ☐ b. a map showing the starting and finish lines of each leg, and checkpoints along the way.
   - ☐ c. radio signals broadcast from the finish line of each leg.

4. Skills needed in past Raid Gauloises events include
   - ☐ a. fishing for sharks and figure skating.
   - ☐ b. pitching, catching, and fielding.
   - ☐ c. rock climbing, kayaking, and biking.

5. During the 1994 race in Borneo, one U.S. team
   - ☐ a. was lost in the jungle for a day.
   - ☐ b. won the event by a full day.
   - ☐ c. got lost and was never seen again.

Score 5 points for each correct answer.

_____ TOTAL SCORE: Recalling Facts

C MAKING INFERENCES

When you use information from the text and your own experience to draw a conclusion that is not directly stated in the text, you are making an *inference*.

Below are five statements that may or may *not* be inferences based on the facts of the story. Write the letter *C* in the box in front of each statement that is a correct inference. Write the letter *F* in front of each faulty inference.

C—Correct Inference   F—Faulty Inference

1. Before each race, the members of each team find out about every hazard along the route.

2. Countries are eager to host the race because being chosen proves that the country is a good place for tourists to visit.

3. Gérard Fusil would be unhappy if newspapers and television networks sent huge news teams to cover the Raid Gauloises and set up news centers along each leg of the race.

4. A smart investor would put money into a resort for beginning mountain climbers at the foot of Mount Tronador.

5. It is possible for an all-woman team to win the Raid Gauloises.

Score 5 points for each correct *C* or *F* answer.

_____ TOTAL SCORE: Making Inferences

D USING WORDS PRECISELY

Each numbered sentence below contains an underlined word or phrase from the story you just read. Following the sentence are three definitions. One is a *synonym* for the underlined word, one is an *antonym*, and one has a completely *different* meaning than the underlined word.

For each definition, write the letter that stands for the correct answer in the box.

S—Synonym   A—Antonym   D—Different

1. If one person drops out, the whole team is <u>disqualified</u>.

____ ☐ a. judged to be suitable

____ ☐ b. popular

____ ☐ c. no longer allowed to win

2. Then they are given maps showing the starting and finish lines of each <u>leg</u>.

____ ☐ a. one section among several

____ ☐ b. whole

____ ☐ c. program

3. But since that means dropping out of the race, flares are always a last <u>resort</u>.

____ ☐ a. obstacle

____ ☐ b. plan

____ ☐ c. place to turn to for help

4. As the hours slipped by, all the Raiders grew weary. Yet they were <u>reluctant</u> to stop.

____ ☐ a. late

____ ☐ b. eager

____ ☐ c. unwilling

5. They <u>staggered</u> along with their backs bent and their eyes sunk in.

____ ☐ a. worked

____ ☐ b. strode

____ ☐ c. tottered

____ Score 3 points for a correct *S* answer.
____ Score 1 point for each correct *A* or *D* answer.

____ TOTAL SCORE: Using Words Precisely

• *Enter the total score for each exercise in the spaces below. Add the scores to find your Critical Reading Score. Then record your Critical Reading Score on the graph on page 114.*

_____ Finding the Main Idea
_____ Recalling Facts
_____ Making Inferences
_____ Using Words Precisely

_____ CRITICAL READING SCORE: Unit 15

Answer Key

1 The Human Fly
Pages 10–15
A. Finding the Main Idea
   1. M   2. N   3. B
B. Recalling Facts
   1. b   2. a   3. c   4. a   5. a
C. Making Inferences
   1. C   2. C   3. F   4. C   5. F
D. Using Words Precisely
   1. a. A   b. S   c. D
   2. a. S   b. D   c. A
   3. a. A   b. D   c. S
   4. a. S   b. A   c. D
   5. a. D   b. A   c. S

2 Bungee Jumping: A Leap of Faith
Pages 16–21
A. Finding the Main Idea
   1. M   2. N   3. B
B. Recalling Facts
   1. b   2. c   3. a   4. a   5. c
C. Making Inferences
   1. C   2. F   3. C   4. F   5. F
D. Using Words Precisely
   1. a. D   b. S   c. A
   2. a. S   b. D   c. A
   3. a. D   b. A   c. S
   4. a. A   b. D   c. S
   5. a. S   b. A   c. D

3 White Water Thrills
Pages 22–27
A. Finding the Main Idea
   1. N   2. B   3. M
B. Recalling Facts
   1. c   2. a   3. a   4. c   5. b
C. Making Inferences
   1. C   2. C   3. F   4. C   5. F
D. Using Words Precisely
   1. a. D   b. S   c. A
   2. a. A   b. D   c. S
   3. a. S   b. A   c. D
   4. a. D   b. A   c. S
   5. a. S   b. D   c. A

4 Hang Gliding: Riding the Wind
Pages 28–33
A. Finding the Main Idea
   1. N   2. B   3. M
B. Recalling Facts
   1. a   2. c   3. b   4. a   5. b
C. Making Inferences
   1. C   2. F   3. F   4. F   5. C
D. Using Words Precisely
   1. a. S   b. A   c. D
   2. a. D   b. S   c. A
   3. a. S   b. D   c. A
   4. a. D   b. A   c. S
   5. a. A   b. D   c. S

5 Climbing the World's Highest Mountains
Pages 34–39
A. Finding the Main Idea
   1. N   2. M   3. B
B. Recalling Facts
   1. a   2. c   3. b   4. c   5. b
C. Making Inferences
   1. C   2. C   3. F   4. C   5. F
D. Using Words Precisely
   1. a. A   b. S   c. D
   2. a. A   b. D   c. S
   3. a. S   b. D   c. A
   4. a. A   b. D   c. S
   5. a. S   b. A   c. D

6 The World's Wildest Horse Race
Pages 42–47

A. Finding the Main Idea
1. B   2. M   3. N

B. Recalling Facts
1. c   2. a   3. b   4. c   5. a

C. Making Inferences
1. F   2. C   3. F   4. C   5. C

D. Using Words Precisely
1. a. D   b. A   c. S
2. a. S   b. A   c. D
3. a. D   b. S   c. A
4. a. S   b. A   c. D
5. a. A   b. S   c. D

7 Skiing the Impossible
Pages 48–53

A. Finding the Main Idea
1. M   2. B   3. N

B. Recalling Facts
1. c   2. b   3. c   4. a   5. b

C. Making Inferences
1. F   2. C   3. C   4. F   5. C

D. Using Words Precisely
1. a. A   b. D   c. S
2. a. D   b. S   c. A
3. a. S   b. A   c. D
4. a. S   b. D   c. A
5. a. D   b. A   c. S

8 Running with the Bulls
Pages 54–59

A. Finding the Main Idea
1. M   2. B   3. N

B. Recalling Facts
1. b   2. a   3. a   4. b   5. c

C. Making Inferences
1. F   2. C   3. F   4. C   5. F

D. Using Words Precisely
1. a. S   b. A   c. D
2. a. D   b. S   c. A
3. a. A   b. D   c. S
4. a. D   b. A   c. S
5. a. A   b. S   c. D

9 Stunt Flying
Pages 60–65

A. Finding the Main Idea
1. M   2. B   3. N

B. Recalling Facts
1. b   2. b   3. c   4. c   5. a

C. Making Inferences
1. C   2. F   3. C   4. C   5. F

D. Using Words Precisely
1. a. A   b. S   c. D
2. a. S   b. D   c. A
3. a. D   b. S   c. A
4. a. D   b. A   c. S
5. a. A   b. D   c. S

10 The Last Great Race on Earth
Pages 66–71

A. Finding the Main Idea
1. N   2. M   3. B

B. Recalling Facts
1. b   2. c   3. a   4. b   5. a

C. Making Inferences
1. C   2. C   3. F   4. C   5. F

D. Using Words Precisely
1. a. D   b. S   c. A
2. a. A   b. D   c. S
3. a. S   b. A   c. D
4. a. D   b. A   c. S
5. a. S   b. D   c. A

11 Conquering Niagara Falls
Pages 74–79

A. Finding the Main Idea
  1. B 2. M 3. N
B. Recalling Facts
  1. b 2. a 3. c 4. b 5. c
C. Making Inferences
  1. C 2. F 3. F 4. F 5. C
D. Using Words Precisely
  1. a. S b. D c. A
  2. a. A b. S c. D
  3. a. A b. D c. S
  4. a. D b. S c. A
  5. a. S b. A c. D

12 Evel Knievel: Motorcycle Maniac
Pages 80–85

A. Finding the Main Idea
  1. N 2. B 3. M
B. Recalling Facts
  1. a 2. b 3. b 4. c 5. a
C. Making Inferences
  1. F 2. C 3. F 4. C 5. F
D. Using Words Precisely
  1. a. A b. D c. S
  2. a. S b. A c. D
  3. a. A b. D c. S
  4. a. A b. S c. D
  5. a. S b. D c. A

13 Buzkashi: War on Horseback
Pages 86–91

A. Finding the Main Idea
  1. M 2. B 3. N
B. Recalling Facts
  1. b 2. c 3. c 4. a 5. b
C. Making Inferences
  1. C 2. C 3. F 4. C 5. F
D. Using Words Precisely
  1. a. D b. S c. A
  2. a. A b. D c. S
  3. a. S b. D c. A
  4. a. D b. S c. A
  5. a. S b. A c. D

14 BASE Jumping: The Outer Edge of Danger
Pages 92–97

A. Finding the Main Idea
  1. N 2. M 3. B
B. Recalling Facts
  1. c 2. a 3. b 4. c 5. a
C. Making Inferences
  1. C 2. F 3. C 4. C 5. F
D. Using Words Precisely
  1. a. A b. S c. D
  2. a. A b. D c. S
  3. a. S b. D c. A
  4. a. D b. A c. S
  5. a. S b. A c. D

15 Raid Gauloises: Ten Days of Hell
Pages 98–103

A. Finding the Main Idea
  1. N 2. B 3. M
B. Recalling Facts
  1. a 2. c 3. b 4. c 5. a
C. Making Inferences
  1. F 2. F 3. C 4. F 5. C
D. Using Words Precisely
  1. a. A b. D c. S
  2. a. S b. A c. D
  3. a. A b. D c. S
  4. a. D b. A c. S
  5. a. D b. A c. S

Words-per-Minute Tables and Progress Graphs

WORDS PER MINUTE

Unit ➤	Sample	1	2	3	4	5	
No. of Words ➤	633	969	1003	981	1092	1045	
1:30	422	646	669	654	728	697	90
1:40	380	581	602	589	655	627	100
1:50	345	529	547	535	596	570	110
2:00	317	485	502	491	546	523	120
2:10	292	447	463	453	504	482	130
2:20	271	415	430	420	468	448	140
2:30	253	388	401	392	437	418	150
2:40	237	363	376	368	410	392	160
2:50	223	342	354	346	385	369	170
3:00	211	323	334	327	364	348	180
3:10	200	306	317	310	345	330	190
3:20	190	291	301	294	328	314	200
3:30	181	277	287	280	312	299	210
3:40	173	264	274	268	298	285	220
3:50	165	253	262	256	285	273	230
4:00	158	242	251	245	273	261	240
4:10	152	233	241	235	262	251	250
4:20	146	224	231	226	252	241	260
4:30	141	215	223	218	243	232	270
4:40	136	208	215	210	234	224	280
4:50	131	200	208	203	226	216	290
5:00	127	194	201	196	218	209	300
5:10	123	188	194	190	211	202	310
5:20	119	182	188	184	205	196	320
5:30	115	176	182	178	199	190	330
5:40	112	171	177	173	193	184	340
5:50	109	166	172	168	187	179	350
6:00	106	162	167	164	182	174	360
6:10	103	157	163	159	177	169	370
6:20	100	153	158	155	172	165	380
6:30	97	149	154	151	168	161	390
6:40	95	145	150	147	164	157	400
6:50	93	142	147	144	160	153	410
7:00	90	138	143	140	156	149	420
7:10	88	135	140	137	152	146	430
7:20	86	132	137	134	149	143	440
7:30	84	129	134	131	146	139	450
7:40	83	126	131	128	142	136	460
7:50	81	124	128	125	139	133	470
8:00	79	121	125	123	137	131	480

Minutes and Seconds ➤

Seconds ◄

	GROUP TWO					
Unit ➤	**6**	**7**	**8**	**9**	**10**	
No. of Words ➤	926	1162	1002	1132	1116	
1:30	617	775	668	755	744	**90**
1:40	556	697	601	679	670	**100**
1:50	505	634	547	617	609	**110**
2:00	463	581	501	566	558	**120**
2:10	427	536	462	522	515	**130**
2:20	397	498	429	485	478	**140**
2:30	370	465	401	453	446	**150**
2:40	347	436	376	425	419	**160**
2:50	327	410	354	400	394	**170**
3:00	309	387	334	377	372	**180**
3:10	292	367	316	357	352	**190**
3:20	278	349	301	340	335	**200**
3:30	265	332	286	323	319	**210**
3:40	253	317	273	309	304	**220**
3:50	242	303	261	295	291	**230**
4:00	232	291	251	283	279	**240**
4:10	222	279	240	272	268	**250**
4:20	214	268	231	261	258	**260**
4:30	206	258	223	252	248	**270**
4:40	198	249	215	243	239	**280**
4:50	192	240	207	234	231	**290**
5:00	185	232	200	226	223	**300**
5:10	179	225	194	219	216	**310**
5:20	174	218	188	212	209	**320**
5:30	168	211	182	206	203	**330**
5:40	163	205	177	200	197	**340**
5:50	159	199	172	194	191	**350**
6:00	154	194	167	189	186	**360**
6:10	150	188	162	184	181	**370**
6:20	146	183	158	179	176	**380**
6:30	142	179	154	174	172	**390**
6:40	139	174	150	170	167	**400**
6:50	136	170	147	166	163	**410**
7:00	132	166	143	162	159	**420**
7:10	129	162	140	158	156	**430**
7:20	126	158	137	154	152	**440**
7:30	123	155	134	151	149	**450**
7:40	118	152	131	148	146	**460**
7:50	118	148	128	145	142	**470**
8:00	113	145	125	142	140	**480**

Minutes and Seconds ➤

Seconds ◄

GROUP THREE

Unit ➤	11	12	13	14	15	
No. of Words ➤	1085	991	1028	952	1156	
1:30	723	661	685	635	771	90
1:40	651	595	617	571	694	100
1:50	592	541	561	519	631	110
2:00	543	496	514	476	578	120
2:10	501	457	474	439	534	130
2:20	465	425	441	408	495	140
2:30	434	396	411	381	462	150
2:40	407	372	386	357	434	160
2:50	383	350	363	336	408	170
3:00	362	330	343	317	385	180
3:10	343	313	325	301	365	190
3:20	326	297	308	286	347	200
3:30	310	283	294	272	330	210
3:40	296	270	280	260	315	220
3:50	283	259	268	248	302	230
4:00	271	248	257	238	289	240
4:10	260	238	247	228	277	250
4:20	250	229	237	220	267	260
4:30	241	220	228	212	257	270
4:40	233	212	220	204	248	280
4:50	224	205	213	197	239	290
5:00	217	198	206	190	231	300
5:10	210	192	199	184	224	310
5:20	203	186	193	179	217	320
5:30	197	180	187	173	210	330
5:40	191	175	181	168	204	340
5:50	186	170	176	163	198	350
6:00	181	165	171	159	193	360
6:10	176	161	167	154	187	370
6:20	171	156	162	150	183	380
6:30	167	152	158	146	178	390
6:40	163	149	154	143	173	400
6:50	159	145	150	139	169	410
7:00	155	142	147	136	165	420
7:10	151	138	143	133	161	430
7:20	148	135	140	130	158	440
7:30	145	132	137	127	154	450
7:40	142	129	134	124	151	460
7:50	139	127	131	122	148	470
8:00	136	124	129	119	145	480

Minutes and Seconds ➤

◄ *Seconds*

READING SPEED

Directions: *Write your Words-per-Minute score for each unit in the box under the number of the unit. Then plot your reading speed on the graph by putting a small* **x** *on the line directly above the number of the unit, across from the number of words per minute you read. As you mark your speed for each unit, graph your progress by drawing a line to connect the* **x***'s.*

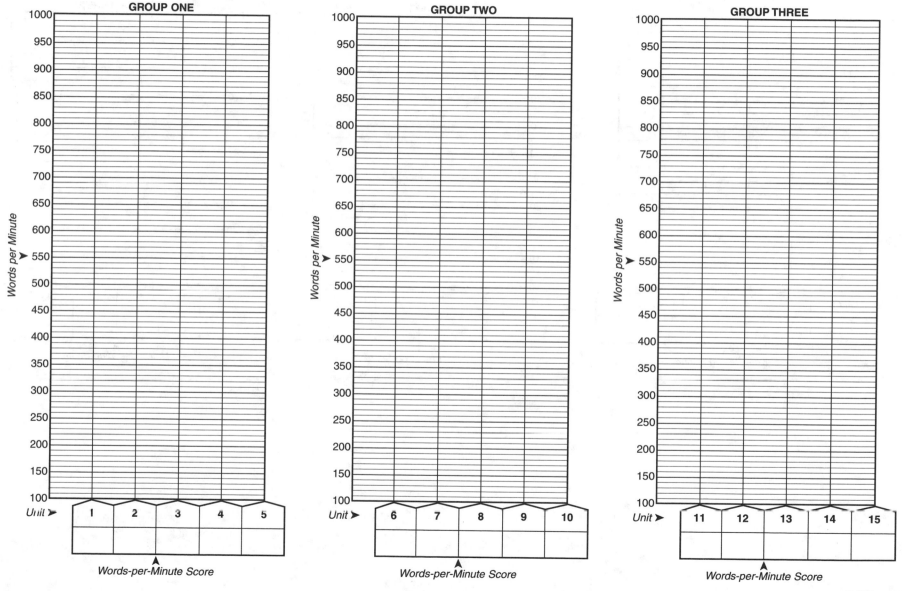

GROUP ONE

GROUP TWO

GROUP THREE

Words per Minute

Words-per-Minute Score

CRITICAL READING SCORES

Directions: *Write your Critical Reading Score for each unit in the box under the number of the unit. Then plot your score on the graph by putting a small x on the line directly above the number of the unit, across from the score you earned. As you mark your score for each unit, graph your progress by drawing a line to connect the x's.*

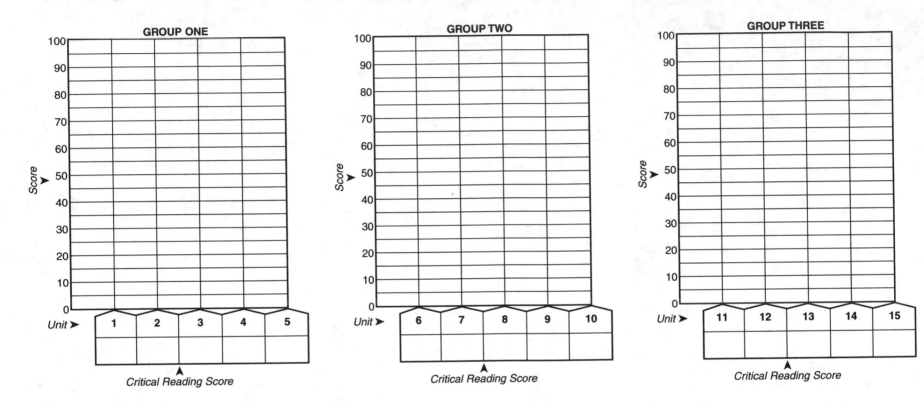

GROUP ONE

Score ➤

Unit ➤   1   2   3   4   5

Critical Reading Score

GROUP TWO

Score ➤

Unit ➤   6   7   8   9   10

Critical Reading Score

GROUP THREE

Score ➤

Unit ➤   11   12   13   14   15

Critical Reading Score